What Others Are Saying About
Master Your Retirement

"Reading *Master Your Retirement* enabled us to understand many of the strategies necessary to plan our retirement, particularly from a taxation perspective. Because we were nearing retirement, it was very relevant to our situation and opened our eyes to the many areas of investment savings to be had by applying the principles in the book to preserve our wealth. Truly timely advice for any age wanting stability with growth. - D. & P. RUDD. LETHBRIDGE, ALBERTA

"If you read one book on retirement, read this one. In this easy to read book, Doug Nelson demystifies all of the key factors that must be addressed in order to *Master Your Retirement*. Highlighting sometimes obvious, but often misunderstood hidden obstacles, such as the Great Killers of Wealth, and identifying our changing needs as we progress through the different phases of retirement, Doug ties it all together by offering a retirement roadmap that ensures you can sleep at night knowing that you are in control of the best stage of your life."
- J. CAMERON STOTT. WINNIPEG, MANITOBA

"*Master your Retirement* is a book for all ages! In fact, the sooner earners of financial resources read this book the better. The financial benefits of doing so can be substantial, in fact, life changing. The book is clearly written, contains a wealth of information and gives concise financial guidance for many stages of life, both pre and post retirement. It is a book that all parents should gift to their adult children - I did!" - J. PETERS. WINNIPEG, MANITOBA.

"A great book that every Canadian thinking of retiring in the next few years, or newly retired should read. It covers all the required subjects, but ties them back to easy to understand case studies. This upd: tance of a financial plan, but also the import: don't go as planned such as the Gre: An easy read that you will t:
- M. LAMONTAGNE. PARTNER. RYAN LAMOI

"*Master Your Retirement* helped me to focus on all financial aspects, what to look for, and the importance of paying attention to the "5 killers of wealth" in order to assure a successful and comfortable retirement. At the end it is important what we keep in our pockets." - A. KONCZ. TORONTO, ONTARIO.

"I have read several excellent books on retirement. I think Master Your retirement by Doug Nelson encompasses everything the others don't. Doug's book is clear and concise and written so that anyone can understand investing and retirement." - B. ELZINGA. CALGARY, ALBERTA

"Doug's straight talk and common sense approach to building wealth and understanding the importance of balance in life is refreshing in an industry that chases overnight success - most often the financial advisor's success. In my opinion, few financial advisors take into account the big picture of what is really important in life and instead over promise and under deliver. Doug's book provides the tools for a real life approach to success, inside and outside of your bank account." - A. DE GAGNE. WINNIPEG, MANITOBA.

"For those who are not fortunate enough to look forward to a gilt-edged retirement pension, *Master Your Retirement* is a must read. Very well written and easy to understand, the detailed information on CPP, OAS and GIS, which almost all Canadians will to some degree benefit from, offers excellent insight into what is available and how to use to your best advantage. With the massive wave of Boomers currently entering their retirement, this book will be extremely useful."
- B. ARBUCKLE. TORONTO, ONTARIO.

Master Your Retirement

How to fulfill your dreams with peace of mind

DOUGLAS V. NELSON
B.Comm.(Hons.), CFP, CLU, MFA, CIM

WINNIPEG, MANITOBA, CANADA

Douglas V. Nelson

MASTER YOUR RETIREMENT - Third Edition
How to fulfill your dreams with peace of mind

Printed and bound in Canada

Library and Archives Canada Cataloguing in Publication

Nelson, Doug, 1967-
Master your retirement : how to fulfill your dreams with peace of mind / Doug Nelson.

Includes index.
ISBN No. 978-1-92749-518-6

1. Retirement income – Canada – Planning. 2. Finance, Personal – Canada. I. Title.

HG179.N45 2008   332.024'0140971   C2008-908024-6

Published by:
Knowledge Bureau, Inc.
187 St. Mary's Road, Winnipeg, Manitoba Canada R2H 1J2
204-953-4769
Email: reception@knowledgebureau.com

Editors: Suzanne Wray and Nicole Chartrand
Cover Design and Layout: Evelyn Jacks and Carly Thompson
Page Design and layout: Karen Armstrong Graphic Design

Table of Contents

Foreword

Why You Need to Read This Book Today

This is a book for people of all ages. It is written for people who don't just want to "do" retirement, but instead, this book is for you if you want to truly "*Master Your Retirement*".

I want you to have it all, whatever this means to you, in your retirement! And so I have written this third edition of *Master Your Retirement* so you can understand, plan and control your wealth with stealth!

I have broken this journey down into several sections:

- **What the Masters Do**: In this first chapter, which is new to the third edition, I will begin by sharing with you traits and strategies already being used by those who are mastering their retirement today.

- **Understanding the Killers of Income and Wealth:** Next, we will reflect on those things that stand in your way of being financially successful. Don't be a victim of the unexpected. We will show you how to identify and stop the erosion of both your retirement income and capital, so you can easily maneuver through the rough waters that will inevitably occur.

- **The Retirement Rules:** What rules do you need to know to ensure you meet your objectives? What rules do you need to know to find the right balance between income, taxes, fees, and portfolio risks? What do you do first, second and third? How do you weigh the pros and cons of various options? How do you select the best combination of investment tools? You see, unless there are some clear "rules" to follow, you will be like a cruise ship sailing across the ocean with no captain and no rudder (and we have all seen recent examples of what can go wrong when this occurs). This, in my view, is one the key reasons why people tend to get into unexpected troubles in retirement. They are either not aware of these important rules, or they fail to follow them over time.

- **The Phases of Retirement:** In this section I will outline for you the five most common phases in retirement and how you can best prepare for each. You will learn how a plan for each can help you maximize even the least enjoyable parts of the journey by knowing what to expect and how to deal with the unexpected. This is all about being forward looking and being prepared. But this is also all about breaking down your retirement years into several smaller stages. Whenever you can break down a larger problem or activity into smaller steps, you always get closer to mastery.

- **The Retirement Mastery Process:** In this section I will encourage you to think in terms of three important processes: i) the month by month mastery process, ii) the income layering process and iii) the portfolio risk management process. You will see how to defeat the sneaky and dangerous Killers of Wealth in each. You will also see why "investment product planning" comes last, after the strategic planning to avoid those killers of your wealth. The portfolio should be designed to deliver the right income at the right time with the least amount of risk and the least amount of tax. The plan for income must always come first. This chapter also talks about reflecting on your current life plan throughout each year. It is always important to have something to look forward to, so living a purposeful life is also key to your success, happiness and peace of mind.

In each chapter of the book, I will provide several practical strategies for you to consider. The ideas and strategies in this book come from over 45 years of real life experience in our family practice. We know what works with families who have experienced retirement. We have found that the best approach, frankly, is to keep it simple.

But before you begin, I wish to add one final point. Like all things in life, the greatest results are achieved with effort. I am not going to promise you that "mastery" will come by putting your retirement plans on auto-pilot or by investing your hard saved money into pre-packaged, financially engineered products that are meant to protect you from all that ails this world.

No, instead I'm going to say that today the world is as it is. It ebbs and it flows, from good times to bad and back again. The current and future markets will always be volatile and uncertain. The economy will always grow and then contract, sometimes lasting for 15 to 20 years at a time. Without question, retirement is a challenge, but this is no different than everything else you have experienced in your life up to now.

If you are looking for the next great investment idea or the next great product solution, this book is not for you. In my experience, there are no quick fix solutions or easy, one-size-fits-all strategies for retirement success. (Sorry to be the bearer of bad news.)

Instead, this book focuses on principles, benchmarks and strategies to:

- Reduce taxation.
- Reduce investment management fees.
- Address head on what we call the "5 Great Killers of Wealth".
- Provide benchmarks for making decisions.
- Break down your retirement years into meaningful stages.
- Identify and manage the risks to your retirement plans today.
- Help you prepare a buffer to all of your decisions.
- Help you create a reliable, consistent and low risk income stream.
- Help you gain the most from your government benefit plans.
- Help you get the most out of your retirement years, bringing you the confidence and peace of mind that you so richly deserve.

While it is nice to think about retirement as a constant period of sunny skies, sandy beaches and unlimited resources, this is far from reality for the vast majority of people. In fact, the struggles you have faced all of your life will often continue into retirement:

- You will worry about your kids and grandkids and will want to support them in any way you can. It is hard for most of us to stop being a parent.
- You will worry about your health and the health of those around you.
- You will worry about your finances and the security of your income.
- You will be hit with unexpected (yet predictable) expenses to maintain your home, your cottage, your vehicles and your travel health insurance.
- As of result, you will have a strong sense of urgency to live for today regardless of the impact this may have in the years ahead. If you string together many back to back years of living for today, you will find over time that you are continuously setting the bar of happiness higher and higher, yet never to be totally fulfilled and potentially closer to financial hardship.
- You will be confident and on top of the world in one moment, and likely frustrated and challenged the next. This will occur time and time again due to constant changes in your finances, your health and your relationships.

How do I know this? I know this because as a financial advisor, and the second generation owner of our family business, we have seen the lives of our clients ebb and flow over the past 45+ years, and I can assure you that this ebb and flow does not stop once you declare yourself retired. There is nothing magical that happens when you enter retirement that suddenly makes you immune to the trials and tribulations of everyday life. The sooner you acknowledge this, the closer you are to mastering your retirement.

What if I told you that you could have:

- Significantly more income in the future, so you could do all the things you most want to do,
- The peace of mind of knowing you can reduce the risk of running out of money in your retirement,
- The confidence of knowing that your portfolio can withstand typical market volatility,

...would you be interested in learning more? I hope so, because these three goals are achievable.

What if you knew you could have hundreds of thousands of dollars more to spend throughout your retirement – without taking on more risk or winning a lottery – would you be interested in reading further? Most people would!

This book is all about achieving real results for you and your family:

- Receiving a consistent and reliable income in retirement (so that you can plan your affairs with confidence).
- Paying the least amount of taxes and fees on your investments (to increase the real value of your income, so you can preserve more of your savings).
- Having a low risk investment portfolio (for peace of mind and reliability of cash flow).

Very simply put, the road to Mastery includes three key points:

Pay Attention to the Details

Pay Attention to the Killers of Wealth

Follow Time Tested Financial Rules and Principles

From my point of view, these three areas are rarely discussed in other retirement planning books or seminars. This is why this book is so important to you today. When you focus on Mastery, you always achieve more. So, don't just "do" retirement, together let's "*Master Your Retirement!*"

Douglas V. Nelson

Introduction

Understanding Today's Retirement Reality

Something is only as good as what you can compare it to. Let's look at some of the most recent retirement statistics, from Canada and around the world.

In the most recent Canadian Census we see:

- The average age in Canada in 2014 is age 58. There are more 58 year olds than any other age group today.

- The baby boom demographic represents 30% of the population in Canada. This group represents those between age 46 and 66 in 2014 (those born between 1946 and 1966). In 2011 the first of the baby boomers reached age 65.

- As the baby boom demographic ages, the growth of the elderly population will begin to accelerate considerably. This will have far reaching changes on our economy. Those age 55 and over will outnumber children within 10 years. This changes the taxpaying base, (fewer taxpayers in the absence of population growth), while at the same time increasing certain social costs, like health care. On the flip side, education and child care costs may change, too.

- One in seven Canadians, or more than four million, are now elderly; two thirds of the very elderly are women. For a variety of reasons, women traditionally have fewer savings than men.

- The average life expectancy of Canadians, which increased appreciably over the past century, is now 82.5 years for women and 77.7 years for men. Retirement for most means a longer period for which income must be planned.

- The proportion of very elderly – aged 80 and over – increased by 25 per cent between 2001 and 2006, second only to the rate of growth of those aged 55 to 64, and surpassed the one-million mark. Age-related disabilities increase for many in the over-80 years, requiring more expensive services, like home care or nursing home care.

According to Statistics Canada you might be surprised to know that of 7.4 million people aged 55 and over, 4.7 million (63.7%) had already retired once. Of this group, 784,000 (17%) returned to work after they "tried out" retirement and found they wanted something different. Approximately 48% returned to some form of work for financial reasons, while others returned to work due to the availability of new, interesting and inspiring job offers. Since the financial crisis, most people have delayed their retirement in order to make up for the ground lost in their portfolios. Unfortunately, this was not possible for those who became sick or were caring for the sick.

This is a serious economic problem for pre-retirees. Of those who did retire,

- 23.7% retired initially due to personal and family responsibilities, often related to family care giving.
- 22.8% retired initially due to personal health concerns.
- Only 19.6% of the group retired because they now qualified for a full pension.

So in as much as you may think you are in control of your future, the reality is that only 20% of those who retired in the last several years did so because they could. Over 45% of Canadians who did retire, did so *for reasons beyond their control.*

All of this information points to the fact that no two retirements are alike and that virtually every retirement is unique (based on the jobs, incomes, pensions, ages, preferences, abilities, health, priorities and interests). To add to this complexity is the fact that both spouses in today's modern age have typically had an income and typically have some form of retirement assets.

These facts have two very significant implications:

- During the working years your family may have access to two to three different sources of income. Yet, in retirement *you could have 15 to 20 different sources of income, each taxed differently and each with different degrees of flexibility.*
- Since both spouses have contributed to family income and family savings, in most situations you are planning for "two retirements" and not just one. This can be good news, from a tax point of view, if it leads to family income splitting but this can also be emotionally challenging when couples strive to determine "what is best".

Consider these real life complexities:

- Each spouse may retire at the same time.
- Each spouse may retire at different times.
- One may retire many years before the other due to a significant difference in age.
- One may wish to travel and volunteer time in the community while the other may wish to stay at home and putter in the yard.
- One may wish to do whatever possible to retire from a stressful current work environment, while the other may have significant retirement goals and plans and can't wait to begin to act on these plans.
- One may be forced to retire gradually, or all at once, due to health issues. The other spouse may wish to retire sooner than planned due to the health care needs of another family member.
- One may retire for a short period of time, only to go back to work again on a part time basis. The other may retire for a short period of time, only to start a small business a few years into retirement.
- One spouse may wish to spend more time with grandchildren, while the other may wish to spend more time with long lost friends.
- One may wish to remain active in a variety of sporting and other social activities while the other may wish to stay close to home and enjoy the tranquility of the garden.

In Canada and around the world we are also seeing many interesting trends:

- The number of "gold plated" pension plans are on the decline. This means that everyone will need to be a better saver and investor. In Alberta alone, it is estimated that only 15% of the population have defined benefit pension plans (i.e. teachers, nurses and other government employees).
- Health care costs for a typical retired couple in the US tops $215,000 (US Bureau of Statistics). While we may not see these expenses directly in Canada, we can still all appreciate that these costs still exist and that someone has to pay for them. These costs will need to be paid, either through taxation or through medical user fees.
- In 2011, over 5 million Canadians contributed to their RRSP (source: Statistics Canada). This is good, but with the average contribution being only $2800; this is nowhere near enough to meet one's retirement goals. Even at a rate of return of 5% per year, over 20 years this contribution level will result in only $92,000 in total savings. At age 65 this would provide only $4000 to $5000 of income per year. This is a good start, but is clearly not enough.

- Recent surveys suggest that as much as 70% of retired people expect to be working in some capacity during their retirement years. Of these people, 29% will work part time for their own enjoyment and may be for no pay whatsoever, 22% will work for additional income, 11% will be running their own business, 6% will work full time doing something completely different and 2% of those surveyed suggested that they had no intention of stopping work at all (Source: Staying Ahead of the Curve, a 2007 National Survey of 1500 workers age 45 to 74). This is the same trend that I see today with my clients.

- Perhaps this trend is suggesting that working beyond age 60 and 65 is becoming a much more accepted norm today and in the future. As people are living longer, many wish to remain active in work for their own enjoyment, fulfillment and feeling of self worth. In a recent UK study, this additional work actually led to greater longevity as well. It is estimated that more than a million people in Britain are now working past the age of 65. The Institute for Economic Affairs (IEA) found that giving up regular work appears to trigger a drastic long-term decline in both physical and mental health. The number of people working past retirement age is growing at a rate of 10% per year. As a result, the number of people accepting early retirement is also on the decline. (Source: Telegraph, UK).

- When we talk about health in an aging population, we also see that Japan has the oldest average age of any country. What is their secret? Would you believe regular exercise? Japan is known as having the greatest "healthy life expectancy". This refers to the number of years that a person can expect to live in good health. In Japan, these figures are estimated to be to age 73, on average, versus age 68 for the US (source: Journal of the American Medical Association). The US ranked 26th out of 34 advanced-economy countries in the study. "Exercise for aging is truly the fountain of youth," said Paula Papanek, program director of the exercise science degree program at Marquette University in Milwaukee. Simply put, those who are more fit in their retirement years live a higher quality of life and spend considerably less on health care related costs, both direct and indirect costs.

With all of this being said, it would appear that an overall "retirement plan" can be hard to nail down. Yet, without a plan, you are like a cruise ship that has no way to steer. You may end up simply adrift for years and years, only to end up like a capsized vessel somewhere off the coast of Italy, which may result in financial turmoil or broken relationships.

But at the same time we are seeing other countries around the world embrace a different view of retirement; a view that includes working in some capacity beyond age 65 and into one's 70's. A view that includes a greater attention to one's health, diet and exercise, not only in retirement but in the years leading up to retirement. One of the key's to a healthy life expectancy is simply to embrace a more healthier you. This is very different than the historical view of a retired person being old, slow and fragile. This is also very different than the traditional notion that "retirement" is a cold turkey event: one day you are working 50 hour weeks and the next you are basking in the sun, only to live happily ever after. It's a nice thought, but a reality that is less and less common.

Yes, for many people, retirement can be the new adventure they have pictured, but it doesn't necessarily come without some well thought out plans that include one's health, exercise and some form of work. These are all things, as we are beginning to see, that contribute to a great, masterful retirement.

With this being said, we then recognize that there are several components to an ideal retirement plan.

- **The Lifestyle Plan:** These are the things you wish to do during your retirement years. This will include your plan for exercise and health, your plan for work and your plan for play. Most retirement plans will also include a series of stages, where each stage may represent 3 to 5 year periods of time. One stage may include more travel whereas another stage may include more time with the grandkids. One stage may include more work for income while another stage may include a greater degree of volunteer activities. All of these components will be considered in your lifestyle plan. The clearer you are on those things that are important to you in your Lifestyle Plan, the more energized and passionate you will be in your life.

- **The After-Tax Income Plan:** This is a breakdown of the after-tax income you will "need" to cover your basic living expenses as well as the additional after-tax income you will "want" so as to meet your lifestyle objectives. This is a technical component of your overall retirement plan that needs to be consistent with your Lifestyle Plan. The first goal is to have a clear understanding of the income you will need each month, after-tax. The second goal is to ensure that you are spending your money in a manner that is consistent with your Lifestyle Plan. Finally, the third goal is to ensure there is no wasted money. You've worked hard to get where you are today, why waste what you've worked so hard to accumulate?

- **The Income Tax and Portfolio Plan:** This is the way in which you will draw the income you need, when you need it, so that you pay the least amount of tax and have the lowest risk portfolio. If you work part time for one or more stages in retirement, this will influence which source of income you draw from first, second and third. This is the critical component that builds the bridge between your Lifestyle Plan and the After-Tax Income Plan.

Since your retirement years will consist of a series of multi-year stages, all three of these plans need to be reviewed every 18 to 24 months. This is how you will gain the most amount of life in each of the years ahead.

Alternatively, your overall retirement plan should never be only about the money and your rate of return. Nor should your retirement plan ignore the money, the portfolio and taxation. That's the first thing you learn when you do retirement planning. You may find that surprising, but it's true.

Sometimes a retirement plan can be hard to nail down because you end up focusing on only one of these areas while ignoring the others. Some people will spend considerable time focusing only on the income tax and the portfolio and forget that they need to plan to live a full and vibrant life. Some people will spend time focusing on the full and vibrant life but be disappointed when the money is not there to fund such a life. Others may ignore both the "after-tax income plan" and the "income tax and portfolio plan" by simply turning on all sources of income at the same time and basing their lifestyle on only what they receive. In this instance, the couple may be paying way too much tax or taking way too much portfolio risk. It will be the taxation and portfolio risk that may ultimately cause them great financial harm in the end.

Retirement means different things to different people, none of which are wrong or inappropriate, they are just different.

To incorporate all aspects of change, you need a strategic retirement plan, your roadmap to navigate your course or a required change of course.

So what is today's retirement reality?

- Your retirement years will consist of a series of stages and transitions. Each stage will last 3 to 5 years in length.
- During one or more of these stages, global trends indicate that you will likely work in some capacity. In some instances this will be for additional lifestyle income while in other situations it may be for additional stimulation and socialization.
- A healthy diet and regular exercise is critical to a healthy, active and dynamic retirement. This adds life to your years while at the same time potentially reducing the risk of additional health care costs.
- Couples need to plan for two retirements, not just one. This approach will help to honor the interests and needs of each spouse over time.

- You will likely have access to 10 or more sources of income throughout your retirement years. The key is determining how best to draw from each source so as to minimize the impact of taxation over time, while also producing a secure income with a lower risk portfolio.

- Finally, today's retirement reality is that retirement is no longer a cold turkey event. For most people, retirement is simply a series of transitions over a longer period of time, as people gradually transition away from full time employment. As a result, the key to Mastery is to be clear about those things of which you are most passionate and to live a joyful life.

IN SUMMARY

Master Your Retirement – Introduction

By following a retirement plan and reviewing it every one to three years you will truly *Master Your Retirement*. You will:

- Adapt to changing circumstances easily,
- Reap the benefits of tax efficiency,
- Live the life you most desire to have,
- Sleep comfortably at night knowing your portfolio has the right risk profile and your basic income needs will always be met,
- Pro-actively plan your future,
- Leave nothing to chance,
- Avoid family conflicts and miscommunication,
- Maximize your lasting legacy for generations to come.

You need to be forward-looking, to anticipate changes before they occur.

Things You Need to Know

- The economy and the stock markets will always be uncertain. Never coast. Never put your retirement plan on "auto-pilot".
- The best way to *Master Your Retirement* is to "focus on the details": learn from the Masters (Chapter 1), defeat the Killers of Wealth (chapter 2) and follow the rules (Chapter 3).
- Government programs are always changing. It is important to stay on top of these changes.
- As our Canadian population ages, more and more pressure will be placed on the health care system during a period when government income from income tax will likely decline. This means that the only constant will be change over your 20+ years of retirement.
- There are three components of a retirement plan: The Lifestyle Plan, The After-Tax Income Plan and the Income Tax and Portfolio Plan.

Questions You Need to Ask

- What are your greatest fears about retirement?
- What would you consider to be the greatest risks of retirement?
- What do you look forward to most about your retirement?
- What does the ideal retirement look like to you?

- To overcome the fears and risks, and to achieve your ideal outcome, how much effort are you prepared to undertake to truly *Master Your Retirement?*

Things You Need to Do

- Be open with your spouse. Talk about the things that you are fearful of and be confident in addressing these issues openly. The worst thing you could do is avoid addressing the difficult issues.
- Be open to learning new things. This will include learning new things about taxes and investments, which may be areas that you are not comfortable with today, but are critical to your long term success.
- Be open to change. Retirement is a long period of time and you and your spouse will evolve during this time.
- Be open to the downside of aging. Aging is for the birds. It is not necessarily a pleasant ordeal to say the least, but it is a reality. To be in denial is to miss opportunities to be with family and friends. To face it head on will result in happier times.
- To minimize the impact of aging and to gain the most from your retirement years, a healthy lifestyle is a critical component of your retirement plan.
- It is becoming the norm to work in some way in the first few years of your retirement.
- Be forward-looking. The single greatest thing you could do to avoid the poor house, is to be forward-looking. This is the process of anticipating future scenarios so that no matter what happens, you are ready.

Decisions You Need to Make

- Will my spouse and I retire at the same time?
- Will we retire at once or will we retire gradually?
- Will we commit to the 12 month plan outlined in Chapter 12?
- Will we commit to trying new things in retirement?
- Will we commit to Mastery?

Mastery Principle

To *Master Your Retirement* is to visualize your retirement three years at a time so that you ensure that you have made plans for all aspects of your life: career, physical activity, health, your spouse, your family and your other relationships.

To have a plan that you are excited about is one of the great contributors to longevity, health and happiness. This is just one of the key differences between people who just "do" retirement, and those who "master" retirement.

1

Lessons from the Masters

"The ultimate measure of a man is not where he stands in moments of comfort and convenience, but where he stands at times of challenge and controversy" MARTIN LUTHER KING JR.

Beth and Cameron are both in their late 50's. The children are grown, have left home and are establishing their own lives, families and careers. For the first time in a long time, Beth and Cameron can begin to focus again on those things that are most important to them.

But where to begin? Beth would love to go back to school, but Cameron would prefer to travel. Cameron wants to spend more time visiting with friends and having them over for dinner, while Beth would prefer to be active in the faith community.

Beth and Cameron have seen some of their friends postpone their retirement years because they simply couldn't agree on what they wanted their retirement to look like. Some postponed their retirement because they were not sure if they had enough money while others clearly stated that they wanted to live for today and figure out the rest later.

Beth and Cameron are not sure if they should be looking to others for advice, or if they should plan a retirement that is unique for them. Then again, Beth and Cameron really hate the entire notion of retirement, because it makes them feel like they are getting old.

Where should they begin?

We have learned many great lessons from those who have created a masterful retirement. Perhaps the greatest lesson of all is that a Masterful Retirement is the next logical extension of a Masterful life. Those who have learned how to create a Masterful Life will also have the most Masterful Retirement. What does this mean?

First, this means that you should toss aside the word "retirement" and whatever you think you are supposed to be doing in retirement. Ignore all of the images provided by the media and even ignore what you see others doing in their retirement years. Instead, focus on what is most meaningful and important to you today and for the next 3 to 5 years. The Masters have taught us that they are most happy when they are living out each phase of their life in ways that are most important to them. They are not living their life by how it has been defined by others. They are living their life, each and every step along the way, on their own terms. Are you living your life on your terms or on the expectations of others?

Second, living a masterful life means that you are proactively and clearly defining each of the next several phases of your life. You are NOT planning for retirement and whatever this means to you. You are NOT planning for a period of decline or aging. Most importantly of all, you are NOT putting your life on autopilot and beginning to coast. Instead, the Masters teach us about the power of continuously planning for all of the phases of your journey called life. When you think of your life as a series of stages, steps or phases, then you see your life as a cumulative, incremental adventure. This is highly energizing, purposeful and meaningful which also creates a higher sense of urgency to each and every day. Do you see your life as a cumulative adventure or are you seeing retirement as your years of decline?

Thirdly, the Masters teach us that the greatest sense of satisfaction and joy often comes when we are in service to others. This means that those who are most happy tend to be those who see the world as a place much bigger than just themselves. This is the value that often comes from work, whether it is for family, for income or as a volunteer. Work, unto itself, is not a bad thing. Instead, work is the foundation of a well-balanced life. The key is to make sure that work is meaningful, empowering and in balance with everything else that is important.

The good news is that this does not mean that you are running yourself ragged. Instead, this means that you are focused, perhaps more so than ever before, on what it means to have a truly balanced and purposeful life.

The true Masters are those who define their life in their own terms, over and over again, year in and year out, in a well-defined and well balanced manner, by spending their time on purposeful and meaningful activities and making adjustments along the way.

THE ISSUES

The problem many of us face today is that we are easily caught up in the challenges of the moment. This may include pressures from family and friends to work, live or act in a certain manner. There may be economic pressures to buy a big home, to move to another big home, to buy a cottage, to take the kids to Mexico each year, to enroll your children in the finest schools or to enroll your children in summer hockey, winter soccer or 6 classes a week at the dance studio. To add to these challenges, you may also be dealing with health issues. This may include aging parents, a sick child or even yourself, dealing with stress, burnout, fatigue or depression. For others, these challenges may also include the ups and downs of running a small business.

To pay for this, and to live the life we most wish to live, most of us need to work really hard. In most situations, this means that both spouses need to be fully employed. While all of the above mentioned goals may be worthy and well justified, the result may be that it leads to a very unbalanced life.

Some of the outcomes of an unbalanced life may be:

- Long working hours that may lead to challenged relationships with your children and your spouse.

- High levels of debt that may lead to increased conflicts about money and feelings of insecurity.

- Long working hours that may limit your ability to have regular exercise, which in turn may result in unhealthy weight gain, which may then lead to current and future health issues.

- Less time spent overseeing your financial affairs and staying in touch with your advisor team. This may mean that your financial plan may be well off track without you knowing. You may also be exposed to unnecessary risks that could cause significant financial harm one day.

- Increased dependency on your current working situation. Any change in this situation could result in a significant disruption to your lifestyle.

The challenges facing today's modern society all stem from the definition of perceived success and happiness. How can anyone possibly be happy unless they "have it all" and "have it all now"? We are bombarded with this same message hundreds of time a day in every form of media.

The problem with this lifestyle pattern, particularly as one moves closer to retirement, is the intensity. As stress levels rise or as health issues begin to emerge, many people feel the need to retire sooner. They know that they can't keep up their current pace. In some cases they know that they just aren't happy and are looking at the utopian view of retirement as their savior. But if their life up to now has been as intense as described above, then odds are they have not had enough time to set aside enough money to leave the work force today. Is this one of the reasons why the savings rate is so low?

In other words, from a financial planning perspective, it is difficult, if not next to impossible to "have it all, all the time". The numbers simply don't add up for most people in most situations.

If these are the statistics for the United States and the so-called land of opportunity, what does this mean to the rest of us?

Ok, enough of this negative stuff, what's the answer?

The answer is clear and simple: Begin today to live a life that has fewer extremes and is in better balance.

Yes, it is clear: life is hard, life has its ups and downs and life is a journey and retirement for many is no different. But, throughout this life, if you pay attention to certain details, you can achieve not only a healthy, balanced lifestyle but also achieve all of the joy, success and happiness you desire. This success doesn't just happen one day, nor does it happen the day in which you retire. Instead, this success, true Mastery, begins today, regardless of your age and stage in life.

The key principles that lead to a balanced, joyful life each and every day are the same principles that apply to a balanced, joyful and masterful retirement. Why save up the best for last? Why be stressed out during your working and family years so that you can one day be hopefully rested and relaxed? Why would we want to jump from one extreme to the next when we can find the right balance today and live this balance each and every year going forward? Why be miserable in your job when you could be excited and passionate about the important work you do each day?

Are most people living a life of extremes, during their working years, so that one day their life could be in better balance (such as in retirement)? Why not look for better balance each and every day and strive to minimize the time spent living in extremes?

The principles and strategies discussed throughout this book are designed to help you find greater purpose and balance in your life.

So who is mastering their retirement today?

We are finding more and more that those who are mastering their retirement today are the same people who have been the masters of their life in the years and decades along the way.

Those who are typically dissatisfied with their work, their relationships or their surroundings during their working years are also those who are typically finding dissatisfaction in their retirement years. Those who found fault with their employers and their working environment are also those who are finding fault and dissatisfaction in their retirement investment portfolios, health care plans and living arrangements.

Alternatively, those who found great joy and abundance during their working and family years, are also those who are finding the same joy and abundance in their retirement years.

These are really important points because many retirement veterans will tell you that retirement isn't always what it's made out to be:

- Your investments rarely perform as you hope.
- More aches and pains arise over time.
- As you age your confidence level declines.
- Travel is becoming more and more expensive and prohibitive.
- Health care and most other living expenses are on the rise.
- The ebb and flow of both the economy and the stock market are of constant concern.
- The adult children of the retired couple will sometimes struggle and call on the retired couple for financial support.

If you are looking toward retirement as the next phase of life to make you truly happy, when you are not happy today, odds are you will find just as many things about retirement that will make you unhappy as you experienced during your working years.

So the key to Mastery is to begin today by creating a well-balanced, focused, meaningful and passionate life, which unfortunately, requires effort.

In the book *Talent is Overrated: What Really Separates World Class Performers from Everyone Else*, author Geoff Colvin states that "the differences between expert performers and normal adults reflect a life-long period of deliberate effort to improve performance in a specific domain". The expert performers focus on a concept called "deliberate practice". In other words, it isn't just a process of working hard, but instead it is a very meaningful and deliberate approach to doing certain things well consistently over time.

What is the deliberate practice we all need to consider today and into retirement?

In Napoleon Hill's *Keys To Success: The 17 Principles of Personal Achievement*, the first and most important principle of success is to "Adopt A Definite Major Purpose". Napoleon Hill describes it as "knowing what you want" so that you can get busy creating it. He encourages you and I to regularly affirm this vision and to see yourself already living this life and to give yourself a compelling motive for doing what you want to do.

Bridging these two thoughts together, if we were to deliberately practice adopting a definite major purpose in our lives, how would that change or influence what you do today and in the future?

To be a Master of your Retirement, you begin by applying those same principles and strategies necessary to create a Masterful life.

THE SOLUTIONS

Who are the Masters and what are they doing? What principles and strategies do the Masters follow each and every day?

The Masters make gradual changes over longer periods of time: The Masters are typically those people who have today, and have always had, mid to longer term objectives or goals. These mid to longer term goals have helped the Masters stay focused on the horizon, and be less worried about some of the smaller details or issues of the day. As a result, their life up to now has rarely experienced a sudden, cold turkey event. Instead, their life has always been a series of gradual changes over longer periods of time. As a result, when they begin to enter their retirement years, the same gradual changes occur as they shift their time and attention gradually from one area to another. The Masters would rarely sell everything and move away to another climate. Instead, due to their outward and strong connection to their community, they may choose to travel to different locations when they so desire to do so. The Masters would rarely leave employment, or a specific job, in one big step. Instead, the Masters would typically transition gradually over a longer period of time. In literally all aspects of their lives, they have been methodical yet purposeful, and so the transition into retirement, for many of the Masters is hardly even noticeable.

The Masters are externally focused: The Masters are those whose passion and interests are typically outward focused on the people and community around them. This may be the creation of specific business oriented or community projects, or it may be a focus on certain charitable desires in Canada or around the world. The focus is typically on something bigger than themselves and lasting for several years at a minimum. This may be an ongoing passion to their Rotary Club (or other service club), their church or their community club. They have skills and experience they wish to share, but most of all they enjoy the connections with others. The Masters are those who view retirement as a time when they can remain externally focused, so they can continue to make a difference and leave things better than how they were found.

The Masters are forward-looking: Very few things in the lives of the Masters happen by chance. In many instances, the Masters will thoughtfully plan their life 6 to 12 months in advance, or around the seasons of the year. They will typically spend time reflecting on the past few years and use these thoughts to influence their direction for the next few years. They want to look back on these years with fondness and pleasure, so they wish to ensure that everything they do is purposeful and meaningful. This brings them great joy and satisfaction, while also ensuring that their money is spent only in those areas that are most important to them today. Some will refer to this as having a "bucket list".

The Masters work as a team: Even though opposites attract, couples who are in alignment work together as a Masterful team in retirement. These couples have found over time ways to honor the interests of the other and provide the necessary time and space for each spouse to do what they each want to do. In essence, they support each other in the activities that are of interest to the other while finding activities they can also do together. Needless to say, this is not always easy, but since many of these things simply evolve over time, the Masters find a way to make it work.

The Masters will quantify the risks and develop a back-up plan: The Masters have learned over their lifetime that unexpected, negative surprises can be often be the most disruptive to a joyful, bountiful life. Therefore, time and attention is spent identifying and quantifying those risks and then developing a back-up plan. By knowing what the back-up plan will be, and by being comfortable that the back-up plan is reasonably adequate, the Masters can then move forward with confidence, and with eyes focused on the horizon. In other words, the Master is less concerned with some of the short term issues, thus reducing their short term worry on situations they cannot control.

The Masters are detail oriented: To build on the previous point, the Masters are also detail oriented. They Masters have learned over their lifetime that the key to their success so far has been their attention to the details. They have learned that their success has come from effort and focus and by avoiding disruptive mistakes along the way. Thus, the Masters take a hands-on, active interest in their affairs to ensure they understand what is taking place and why different types of recommendations are being considered. The Masters will seek advice from others and then size up this advice so as to make their own decisions. The Masters are not frivolous with their money, instead they are very purposeful. They recognize the value of a dollar and do all they can to stretch it as far as possible for the greatest possible benefit, for themselves, their family and / or their community. They know how much their taxes are. They know what their expenses are. They know what they need to make things work and they know how much more money they need to do all the things they want. The Masters never use the excuse that something is too difficult or complicated to understand. If they don't understand something, they spend time learning it.

The Masters never stop learning: The Masters are those with an enduring appetite for learning and a continuous interest in the world around them. They are naturally inquisitive. They want to understand how things work and why things happen the way they do. While they have their opinions of the world, they are mostly interested in observing the world around them with curiosity and interest as to how things may unfold. Their life experience tells them that the world will adapt and it will change over time, sometimes for the good and sometimes for the bad. They recognize and accept that you can't have the good without the bad and so they take the ebb and flow of life as it comes, with confidence. Many Masters will then take these insights and spend time with younger people in their family and their community, helping to transition these great lessons of life to the next generation. As Ben Franklin was quoted as saying, *"when you're finished changing, you're finished"*. The Masters are never finished.

These seven principles will be reinforced time and again throughout each of the chapters in this book. However, pay particular attention to the themes of each of these chapters as it relates to each of these seven principles. The order below is based on the order of the chapters:

- Chapter 2 (The Great Killers of Wealth) and Chapter 3 (The Principles and Rules To Master Your Retirement) emphasize many of the important details on which to focus (Principle 6).

- Chapters 4 and 5 provide many other important details to consider, but they also emphasize the importance of being forward-looking, anticipating changes before they occur and planning ahead. Chapter 4 introduces the notion of the 5 Phases of Retirement while Chapter 5 illustrates important considerations when you are 7 to 10 years away from retirement. These chapters are great examples of Principle 3: Be Forward-Looking and Principle 6: Be Detail Oriented.

- Chapter 6 and Chapter 8 introduce a process to developing a retirement vision and lifestyle plan for the next 3 to 5 years. These chapters emphasize many of the thoughts found in this chapter as well as Principle 2 above: the importance of being externally focused, Principle 4: Working as a team and Principle 7: Never stop learning.

- Chapters 7 reviews many of the important details to focus on during the first two years of retirement, but it also emphasizes the importance of not making any major decisions or life changes during these first two years. This is consistent with Principle 1: Making Gradual Changes Over Longer Periods of Time.

- Chapters 9 through 12 especially reinforce Principle 5: the importance of identifying future risks and developing a back-up plan. These chapters discuss anticipating inevitable changes to your retirement plan as you age. These chapters also reinforce Principle 3 (Be Forward-Looking).

- Chapter 13 summarizes steps that can be taken throughout the year to create a Masterful plan in Retirement. Chapter 13 emphasizes each of the seven principles discussed here in Chapter 1.

When we think of retirement, we typically think of a stress free life, doing all the things we want to do whenever we want to do them, having money in the bank while receiving a continuous, secure and abundant income that grows with inflation over time. While this type of retirement may happen for some, it certainly does not happen for the majority. As a result, the financial services industry has, time and time again, developed product solutions that are designed to deliver this type of comfort, peace and security. Yet, in my experience, these products rarely pan out as desired, which leads me to believe that we cannot financially engineer our way to success and mastery. Instead, we need to begin with the realization that there is no golden solution that will work perfectly for all people in all situations at all times. We also need to realize that neither you nor I can put 20+ years of retirement on autopilot and expect everything to work out. We cannot create one plan today and expect that plan to be the ideal approach each and every year for the next 20+ years. Instead, we always need to review and update our plans each and every year over time.

To review these plans, it is helpful if not even necessary to begin by identifying what it means to live a well-balanced, masterful life in retirement.

- What does this ideal, well balanced, purposeful life look like to you today?
- How much time are you working?
- What type of work are you doing? What type of work do you most enjoy?
- Are you exercising regularly?
- Do you have other activities you enjoy that keep you active?
- How much time will you spend with friends and family?

- How much time will you be travelling?
- Will you be studying a new subject or taking classes to learn a new skill (i.e.: like learning a new language or taking a cooking class)?
- Will you be volunteering your time?
- What activities, events or situations are you most passionate about?

When you have a picture of what a well-balanced, moderate, masterful life looks like for you today, or during a specific phase of your retirement years, then you are more likely to know when your day to day has gone off track. You are also likely to know more quickly when things begin to get off track. Remember, something is only as good as to what you can compare it to. Having a picture of a moderate, masterful life is one of the keys to ensuring that your financial plan is consistent with this ideal life.

You see, when you are clear on the answers to the above questions, then there is also greater clarity on how your financial affairs should be structured, how your taxes can be minimized, how and when you should begin to draw your Canada Pension Plan retirement benefits and how your portfolio should be structured. When you have greater clarity on how your financial affairs should be structured, you will now be able to determine where the risks lie in your plan and what you need to do to protect against these risks. You will also be able to see the extent to which you have a "buffer" to your current plan, so that you can absorb with ease the typical ups and downs that will occur over time. Remember, throughout your retirement you will move through several stages and so how you answer these questions will likely evolve over time. This means that how and when you draw from each different source of income will need to change over time as well.

IN SUMMARY

Lessons from the Masters

To get the results in retirement that you desire, you will need to focus your time and attention on certain things throughout the year, each and every year. But here is the good news. These things don't take much time, yet the results can be exponential.

It is with this in mind that we reflect on this notion of Mastery.

Those who are mastering his or her retirement today are those who are also mastering their life in their pre-retirement years. Those who are mastering his or her retirement today are those who are focusing their time and attention on the seven principles and strategies of mastery described earlier in this chapter.

The rest of this book will explore these seven areas in more detail.

Things You Need to Know

- Most people will transition into retirement gradually over time.
- Your life up to now has always consisted of a series of stages or phases. Your life going forward will continue to be a series of stages and phases.
- The best plans are those that are 3 to 5 years at a time.
- Life is a cumulative journey of experiences, relationships and learning. The most successful Masters in retirement are those who continue to accumulate and grow in each of these areas.

Questions You Need to Ask

- Do you relate to the seven principles unique to those who are Mastering their Retirement today?
- Which of the seven principles do you relate to the most and why?
- Which of the seven principles are most concerning to you and why?
- Are your expectations about retirement, or the next phase of your retirement years, realistic?

Things You Need to Do

- Define what a well-balanced, meaningful life looks like to you. Create a weekly, monthly and seasonal schedule of your activities and events and then reflect on this schedule makes you feel.
- Compare these notes with how you are living your life today. Are you living a hectic life of extremes? If so, what would you change so that you could move closer to your "benchmark lifestyle" defined above?
- Prepare a game plan 2 to 4 years in advance that will help you gradually move out of the extreme activities you find yourself in today and move towards your ideal, balanced lifestyle.
- Identify the risks associated with your current and ideal plan.
- Identify a "buffer" so that you know what your game plan is if things don't work out as planned.

- Are you prepared to spend a modest amount of time focusing on the details of your own financial affairs or would you prefer to put your financial plan on auto-pilot?

- Are you prepared to create a forward-looking lifestyle plan that you can be excited about?

- Are you prepared to spend some time thinking about the "definite major purpose" of your life over the next 3 to 5 years?

Mastery Principle:

A Masterful Retirement is a purposeful and focused retirement. Yet, a Masterful Retirement is really just an extension and another phase of a Masterful Life. A Masterful Life is based on a "definite major purpose" that is backed up by the "deliberate practice" of important strategies (as we will discuss throughout this book).

2

The Great Killers of Wealth

"It does not matter what you have, it only matters what you keep: after-tax, after-fees and after-inflation." EVELYN JACKS

Thomas and Richard were playing golf together the other day. As lifelong friends, their conversation inevitably shifted to investments and retirement. Thomas was feeling a little frustrated, not only because his game was not as good as it could have been that day, but because his retirement scenario was not panning out as well either. "I can't believe that I've worked so hard all my life, always trying to do the right things financially, yet when it comes to retirement, the person who will receive the least amount of my hard earned savings is me!"

"What do you mean?" asked Richard.

"By the time I pay investment management fees and income tax", said Thomas, "more than 50% of my rate of return will be gone! If my investments earn an 8% return, the first 2.5% disappears in fees, resulting in a net return of 5.5% to me. If I drew this amount out in income, 30% of this amount would disappear in tax. This means that I'm living off of an investment return, after-tax and after-fees, of about 3.85% when my investments actually earned 8%! I'm living off of less than half of what my investments actually returned!"

Richard thought about this for a moment and then asked Thomas "so what does your investment advisor say about this?"

Thomas laughed. "My investment advisor tells me that I need to take more risk with my investments if I want to have more income to live on." This was the last thing that Thomas wanted to do. "I never realized that taxes and investment fees", Thomas concluded, "could destroy my hard earned income and capital so quickly. What is one to do?"

THE ISSUES

In Chapter 1 we stated that the retirement years can be challenging for many reasons, such as those issues mentioned above by Thomas. We also talked about the fact that the Masters are those who pay attention to certain key and important the details over time (Principle 6). Many of the most important details that need attention relate to your taxes, investment management fees, inflation, interest costs and market volatility. In this chapter, we refer to these items as the Great Killers of Wealth, which is often the source of most people's frustrations throughout their retirement years. To be a Master, it is critical to apply the principles of "deliberate practice" by consistently reviewing the impact of these Great Killers of Wealth on your current situation.

In this chapter we will explore the impact of the Great Killers of Wealth and how to address them head on, each and every day, so as to create higher probability outcomes in retirement. This chapter contains a lot of numbers, so I encourage you to go slow and make some notes so that you can see just how significant the Great Killers of Wealth can be throughout your retirement years.

To begin this discussion, many retirement commentators will speak about issues such as the long term risk of running out of money, but this is the equivalent of putting the cart before the horse. The real issue is what I call the "Killers of Wealth" – taxes, fees, interest costs, inflation and market volatility. The Great Killers of Wealth impact everything:

- Having the ideal amount of income today.
- Having the ideal amount of income tomorrow.
- Protecting purchasing power over a long period of time.
- Having capital available for emergencies or medical needs.

Addressing each of these Great Killers of Wealth is critically important to Mastering Retirement.

Let's consider the impact of each.

1. Tax

Simply put, tax is life's single greatest expense. Many individuals will have an average tax rate of 25% to 30% throughout retirement. For an average individual, with a total retirement income of $60,000 and a 20% average tax rate, this could result in annual taxes of $12,000. Over 25 years of retirement, this could easily work out to be $300,000 or more in personal income taxes paid throughout their retirement years.

When you think about your RRSP or Pension plan, 20% to 40% of this plan value may ultimately disappear in taxes, either during the years when you are drawing income or in your final estate (when you are deceased). So what you have, in either income or capital, is not what you will keep. It is shocking to see just how much of your hard earned, and hard saved money will disappear in tax, in one way or another.

2. Investment Management Fees

The day you retire may be the day on which you have the greatest amount of life-time wealth. A typical mutual fund today has an annual investment management fee that is 2.5% of the value of your investments. This amount is charged each and every year. If you have $500,000 of investment savings, this is an annual expense of $12,500. Over a 25 year period of time, this works out to be $312,500 in fees paid.

It is important to note that these also incur GST and/or HST, depending on your province of residence, or the province in which the investment is managed. An additional 5% GST on $312,500 is $15,625. A 13% HST is $40,625 in additional expense.

There are also many investment products today that provide additional "guarantees" that help to protect the investor from running out of money. Unfortunately, many of these products cost as much as 1% of the value of the investment per year above and beyond the fees mentioned above. Based on your $500,000 in savings, this could be an additional $5000 per year (plus 13% HST =$5650). Over a 25 year retirement period, this works out to an additional expense of $141,250.

Therefore, if the investment fees are an average of 2.5%, plus a 1% guarantee fee, plus 13% HST, $500,000 in investment savings could end up paying close to 4% in total annual fees. Over 25 years of retirement, this is an approximate total cost of $500,000 in investment management fees paid, on your $500,000 investment.

Now, where does this money really come from? This is the money that is drawn from your investment account each and every year by the money manager. Over the past 25 years, the average Canadian Balanced Equity Fund produced a return of 6.4% after-fees, based on an average MER (Management Expense Ratio) of 2.52% (source: Morningstar Paltrak Software, for the period ending July 31, 2013). This means that the before fee return would have been 8.92%. The fees paid, in this case, represent 28% of the total rate of return. By comparison, a "passive balanced investment" (40% short term bond index, 30% Canadian equities, 30% global equities) produced an average annual return of 7.8%. Much of the difference in these rates of return is the fees.

For the balanced fund to earn an "after-fee" return of 7.8%, it actually needs to earn a before fee return of 10.32%. To achieve this higher return, the fund manager must take on more risk, which means your portfolio is more volatile and the risk of losing capital due to the combination of income withdrawals and negative rates of return is greatly enhanced. Yet, if the passive investment earned a 7.8% return and we subtract out the fees of 4%, the real after-fee return may end up being only 3.8%. In other words, the higher the fees, the more difficult it is for the money manager to generate the rate of return you may need to meet your goals. This also means the money manager must take on more and more risk just to overcome the fees.

In retirement, investment management fees are one of the Great Killers of Wealth because at this stage in life you have the most amount of money to invest. Over a long retirement period, this can result in hundreds of thousands of dollars of fees paid that ultimately result in lost return. The lower the return, the less capital you have and the more likely you will run out of money.

3. Inflation

Inflation is purchasing power. For a growing economy, inflation of 1% to 3% each year is a good thing because it tells us that our economy is growing. However, when inflation begins to exceed 3%, the concern is that inflation will begin to get out of control and rise to higher and higher rates.

Over a 25 year period of time, a 2% rate of inflation will reduce the value of your purchasing power by approximately 40%. In other words, the $500,000 you have invested when you retire will be the equivalent of $300,000, 25 years down the road. The $25,000 of investment income your $500,000 portfolio generates will be the equivalent of $15,000, 25 years down the road. For you to maintain your purchasing power over a long retirement period, your portfolio and/or your after-tax income needs to grow by 2% per year.

With this being said, a portfolio that earns an 8% return before taxes, fees and inflation is used up very quickly. The first 2.5% may disappear in fees, leaving an after-fee return of 5.5%. The next 30% is paid in tax, leaving you with 3.85% on which to live. Yet, to offset inflation you should really draw only 1.85% of this value for income. So of your 8% gross rate of return, only 1.85% should be used for after-tax income needs.

Obviously, this is a problem that needs to be addressed, which we will. But before we do that, we need to look at the last two Killers of Wealth.

4. Compounded Interest Costs

If you have debt, you are paying interest costs to maintain this debt. Over time, this can add up to a considerable expense. The classic example is of someone who "downsizes" their home in retirement, yet ends up with a small mortgage. Even a mortgage of $100,000, paid off over 10 years in retirement (assuming an interest cost of 5%), will result in $28,000 of interest costs. Yet, these interest costs are paid with after-tax money. Therefore, you will need to withdraw $39,000 from your RRSP or pension plan so that you can pay $11,000 in taxes and $28,000 in interest costs.

Debt, particularly in a rising interest rate environment, is a Great Killer of Wealth. In this simple example, the debt cost increased the total purchase price by close to 40%, when measured on a before tax basis. Paying down debt during retirement is an extremely expensive event.

5. Market Volatility

The last of our Great Killers of Wealth is market volatility. Volatility is the degree to which your investment will fluctuate over time, while you draw income from the investment. Market volatility can be a Great Killer of Wealth when your portfolio suffers from either a low return or a negative return, at a time when you are also drawing income from the investment. It is the combination of these two factors that results in a loss in your hard earned savings. It is important to realize that this loss is something from which you may never recover.

Consider the following two examples.

Example 1: Your $500,000 portfolio generates a before tax, after-fee return of 2%. Your planned income withdrawal is the equivalent of $25,000 (5% of the value of the portfolio). This is a net return of -3%. While you started the year with $500,000, you have ended the year with $485,000. In the following year you draw the same $25,000. To get back to the $500,000 level your investment return, after-fees, needs to be as high as 9%. Remember, this is an after-fee return, which means that your investment needs to earn 11.5% or more. The question is: how much risk does the portfolio have to take to create this higher return?

Example 2: Things are even worse if you have a negative return of -5%. At the end of the year your $500,000 portfolio may be worth only $450,000. To get back to the $500,000 level you need to earn a one year return, after-fees, of closer to 12%. Before fees, your return needs to be closer to 14.5% or more.

In other words, the odds of recovering your capital when you suffer the combined impact of a negative return with an income withdrawal are very low. As a result, "market volatility" in retirement is not your friend. It is something that can destroy wealth quickly if you are not careful and prudent. There is no glory in portfolio risk in retirement. I will provide you with some ideas on how to manage portfolio risk in Chapter 12.

My hope is that you can clearly see that the combination of taxes, fees, inflation, interest costs and market volatility, the Great Killers of Wealth, can easily destroy your hard earned savings. Eliminating the negative impact of each of these factors is a critical key to Mastering Your Retirement. This is why paying attention to these details is so critically important to your financial success.

THE SOLUTIONS

The solutions to the Great Killers of Wealth are really quite simple: pay less tax, pay lower investment management fees, manage your debt prudently, build an investment portfolio that contains investments that are most likely to grow during the current market environment and adopt strategies that minimize the risk of losing capital. Throughout the rest of this book we will explore many ways to achieve these outcomes. Below is a short list of the most important concepts, each of which will be explored in greater detail in the coming chapters.

Pay Less Tax

There are several ways to pay less tax on your income in retirement:

- **Be aware of how different types of income will be taxed in retirement**. Your income in retirement will be a combination of 10, 15 or more different sources of income, where each source of income will fall into one of three categories: i) income that is fully taxable, ii) income that is partially taxable, and iii) income that is not taxable. To begin, make a list of all possible sources of income in retirement. Next, determine the extent to which each source is taxed (see the table in chapter 5)

- **Be aware of the "three key tax zones"**. There are three key tax zones on the tax return for those aged 65 and older (discussed in more detail in Chapter 7). To minimize tax in retirement, be aware of the three key tax zones.

- **Split income equally between spouses**. Two smaller, but equal, incomes will always pay less total tax than one large income and one small income.

- **Plan your income sources pro-actively**. In the 10 years leading up to retirement, it is prudent to plan your income sources pro-actively so that you will have the right amount of income coming from the right sources so as to minimize tax on the income received (more on this in Chapter 5).

- **Measure your tax picture twice annually**. Twice a year it is prudent to measure your tax picture. In April of each year, when you prepare your tax return, you are able to see the impact of all of the decisions made in the previous year. You will be able to clearly identify where you need to make changes to your income plan so as to have a better result for the current year. Then, in November, prepare a preliminary tax return for the current year, based on the current years expected income and deductions. This will give you important insight into ways in which you could reduce tax for the current year and identify ways in which you could reduce tax in future years. In other words, if you look at your tax picture only in April each year, it will be too late to make any end of year improvements and, as a result, you will have paid too much tax (more on this in Chapter 12).

Reduce Investment Fees

There are many ways to reduce investment fees:

- **Be aware of what you are paying today**. The first step is awareness. What fees you are paying today and how does this compare with other alternatives? After all, something is only as good as what you compare it to.

- **Be aware of all the alternative investment choices**. All investment advisors must hold a license to sell an investment product to the public. The license the investment advisor holds determines the investment options they will recommend to you. As a rule of thumb, I recommend you find a licensed investment advisor who is able to provide the widest range of investment options.

- **Be aware of guarantees**. The cost for many investment products rise considerably when "guarantees" are added to the product. Obviously, since there is no free lunch, these guarantees have a cost which, over time, can add up to a considerable amount of money. The firm that provides the guarantee must collect enough money to provide this service at a profit. When calculating the amount to charge for this guarantee, the firm will also determine the odds of someone making a claim against the guarantee. Of the people who pay for the guarantee, only a small number will be in the position to ever make a claim against the guarantee. Therefore, it is important to recognize that only a small number of people, perhaps as low as 5% to 15% of the participants will actually make a claim which also means that 85% to 95% of the people who buy the product because of the guarantees, will never benefit from the money paid for the guarantee. Therefore, is the guarantee really worth it? Another way to look at it is to look for ways in which you could reduce the "risks" the guarantee strives to address, and thus not spend the money on the guarantee itself. There is always more than one way to manage a risk or achieve an objective.

- **Choose lower risk investment options**. There is "no glory in taking investment risks in retirement" (More on this in Chapter 12). In other words, the odds of "running out of money prematurely" is greatly enhanced when you take more portfolio risk in retirement, while at the same time drawing income from the portfolio. Frankly, one of the best ways to reduce investment management fees is to choose lower risk investments. Lower risk investments also don't need to have "guarantees" that add to the cost of your portfolio.

- **Lower risk investment options often come with lower fees**. As a result of all of the points made above, a lower risk, income-oriented portfolio, responsible for generating up to 30% of the annual income will result in an investment mix that is considerably more conservative than what most people would have in their investment portfolio today.

As a result, this type of portfolio approach achieves three things: i) the fees could be as much as half of a typical balanced mutual fund, ii) the volatility is considerably less and iii) the types of securities held in the portfolio can play a role in offsetting the long term effects of inflation.

Managing Debt

In today's environment we have very, very low interest rates. In the coming years many people expect to see interest rates rise. Interest rates, just like the economy and the stock market, will rise and fall over time. The long term average interest cost for loans in Canada has been approximately 7% over the past 40 years. Over the past 20 years interest rates have been "below the long term average". Many people expect to see a period where interest rates will be above the long term average, similar to what we saw in the 1970s.

There are two trigger events for this scenario:

- **Global government debt:** Today many governments around the world, including industrialized nations such as Britain, Japan, the US and even Canada (if we're not careful), are reaching levels whereby the debt they have incurred is reaching a tipping point. A tipping point is reached when the debt is growing faster than the economic growth of the country. If it is perceived that the government is not able to maintain its obligations to its debt holders, then the "risk of default" on that debt goes up. The interest rate is the indicator of risk and is determined by the buyer of the debt rather than the seller. This means nations with considerable debt do not have control over their interest rates. The more debt they owe, the higher the interest rate the borrower will insist on receiving and, as a result, the consumer will see interest rates rise in their country.

- **Inflation**: The second trigger to higher interest rates is inflation. In order to make it easier for governments to pay down their debt, they can create inflation which results in the value of yesterday's debt declining in relation to the value of the currency today. There are typically three ways to get out of a "debt crisis": i) raising taxes, ii) reducing government expenses and iii) creating inflation. In time, governments will need to raise interest rates so as to keep inflation under control. If there is too much inflation then the economy could get into significant trouble. Therefore, the central bank will (hopefully) raise interest rates so as to keep inflation under control.

Managing Inflation and Designing the Portfolio

Inflation is an important component of a healthy economy, when it is kept in check. Many advisors would suggest that you need to increase your exposure to the stock market, in your investment portfolio, so as to offset the risks of inflation over time. While this point, in general, is true, it is not the whole story and here's why:

- A rising inflationary environment typically results in higher interest rates.
- When interest rates go up, the value of many "defensive, interest bearing investments" goes down. This means that bonds, and bond funds, will go down in value in a rising interest rate environment.
- If interest rates go up, the cost of borrowing capital for businesses also goes up. This means that the "profit" for most companies will likely go down in this environment. Therefore, the stock value, and the stock market in general, will also eventually decline.

For at least some of the rising interest rate/rising inflation period, hard assets tend to hold their value. This would include direct exposure to gold, silver, copper (and other industrial metals), agricultural commodities as well as real estate. These commodities may produce a higher return until such time as the price of these items rises to a level that is unsustainable. We refer to this level as the point of "demand destruction", when the price of the commodity ultimately destroys the demand for the item. At some point, this may occur and so it is prudent to remain attentive to this.

Another investment option is a "real return bond". This is an inflation protected bond whereby both the value of the bond and the interest paid rises with the rate of inflation each year.

You could construct a very defensive portfolio that "tilts" towards these items and thus protects your portfolio from inflationary pressures. So, it is not just having exposure to stocks that will protect you from inflation, but rather it also relates to which stocks, or commodities, you own in your portfolio. This, of course, makes things that much more complicated, which is why I recommend you don't rely too heavily on your investment portfolio to produce a regular income in retirement. I do suggest you consider the 30% test, described in more detail in Chapter 3.

So, to protect against inflation, hold those investments inside your portfolio that will typically rise in a higher inflation/rising interest rate environment. Don't assume that the portfolio that made money for you yesterday will get you to where you wish to go in the near future.

IN SUMMARY

The Great Killers of Wealth

The best and easiest way to receive a safe and secure retirement income is to avoid those things that can ultimately "kill your wealth" over time. We live in an after-tax, after-fee and after-inflation world, yet most of the time both the media and advisors speak to you from both a before tax and a before fee point of view. We have learned that the only thing that really matters is the money you have left over to spend each month. Therefore, focusing on the "Great Killers of Wealth" is the most important component to growing and protecting both your income and your capital over your lifetime. From the examples shown in this chapter, we know that these issues could cost you several hundred thousand dollars which ultimately take away from your income and lifestyle in retirement.

Things You Need To Know

- The amount of tax you are paying today.
- The fees you are paying today.
- The risk profile of your portfolio today.
- The debt costs you are incurring today.

Questions You Need To Ask

- What do I need to do to pay less tax?
- What do I need to do to pay fewer fees?
- Am I paying for guarantees? If so, what are they and how important are they to me?
- What do I need to do to reduce my long term interest costs?
- What do I need to do to have a lower risk portfolio?
- What investment products is my investment advisor licensed to provide and what investment products is he/she not licensed to provide?

Things You Need To Do

- Determine an alternative tax and investment fee structure with which you are comfortable.
- Determine the amount of annual savings and then multiply this amount over the remaining term of your retirement years. If you are 65 today, use 20 years as your life expectancy.
- Work with a tax advisor who can help you optimize your tax return.
- Work with a financial advisor who will work with both you and your tax

advisor to determine the most efficient way to structure your portfolio so as to produce the most tax-efficient income stream.

Decisions You Need To Make

- Commit to slaying the Killers of Wealth.
- Determine if your tax advisor is in sync with your goals.
- Determine if you need to expand your advisor team to include others with different licenses and/or skill sets.
- Commit to reviewing the Killers of Wealth annually so as to always ensure none of your hard earned money is going to waste.

Mastery Principle

Be aware of the Killers of Wealth. When you are able to lower your taxes, reduce your fees, reduce investment risk, invest into securities that will grow in an inflationary environment and avoid long term interest costs, you will be well on your way to having the income you want in a low risk manner. It's just that simple. But you have to pay attention to the details.

3

The Principles and Rules to *Master Your Retirement*

"The great performers isolate remarkably specific aspects of what they do and focus on just those things until they are improved; then it's on to the next aspect." GEOFF COLVIN

Marlene and Michel are overwhelmed at the number of choices relating to their retirement:

- *Which pension option should they choose?*
- *Should they convert their RRSP to a RRIF now or later?*
- *How much income should they draw from the RRIF?*
- *Should they take their Pension Plan retirement benefit now or later?*
- *How much risk should they take in their investment portfolio?*
- *What should they invest their money into?*

Should they buy additional insurance products such as long term care insurance and what on earth is a GMWB?

They have been planning their retirement for several years now and yet the answers to these questions are not any clearer today than in the past. They have met with different advisors who all provide different answers.

Yes, Marlene and Michel are overwhelmed and unsure of where to turn.

If only there were some guidelines to follow.

THE ISSUES

Retirement IS complex for many reasons. This is a very significant time in your life when your income now comes from investments rather than from work. You are transitioning from one or two sources of income to as many as 15 to 20 different sources of income. During your working years your income was taxed in a straightforward manner, whereas in retirement, different sources of retirement income may be taxed in different ways.

Yes, retirement IS complex. It is with this in mind that we reflect on Principle 3 discussed in Chapter 1: Be Forward-Looking. This is one of the most powerful and important components lived out by the Masters. To be forward-looking means that you need to anticipate the various phases that you may go through during your retirement years.

Compounding this complexity are the typical questions, many of which are listed above, that face retirees. Marlene and Michel's experience is not unlike many others whereby the answers to these questions will vary depending on with whom they speak. Unfortunately, the answer they will receive from different advisors is often greatly influenced by the product licenses held by each advisor.

To be clear, this is not to say that advisors are providing inappropriate advice. Yet, I do wish to suggest that the advice provided is naturally influenced by the tools available.

You see, in virtually everything in life, including the financial services business, the advice you receive is always dependent on the tools, knowledge and bias of the person providing the advice. While the advice provided may not be bad advice, you may be able to achieve the same or greater benefits through an alternative approach. During the retirement years, every dollar counts. As we see in the chapter on the Great Killers of Wealth, hundreds of thousands of dollars are in play. With this in mind, what rules or principles should one consider to enhance the probability of success? This purpose of this chapter is to present a series of principles and rules to follow when planning for retirement and for making ongoing decisions throughout retirement. The rules will help to answer the questions plaguing Marlene and Michel while also overcoming the Killers of Wealth.

Before we move on, let's bridge these thoughts back to Chapter 1. The Masters are those who make gradual changes over time. But to make these gradual changes, it is important to know what changes need to be made and why. To answer these questions, it is necessary to develop some Principles and Rules to follow over time so that decisions can be made consistently and confidently. The Masters will also quantify the risks to their current plan. The Principles and Rules that follow help to measure where these risks are and how they can be addressed. This is the type of detail that is necessary to ensure that things stay on track over time.

The Masters are those who deliberately practice these Principles and Rules until such time as they are perfected. Once perfected, the Masters focus on other details so that these cumulative efforts create consistently positive results.

THE SOLUTIONS

Principle 1: Focus on "Income" First Then Capital

Retirement is all about the income. The money we receive from government benefits, pensions and investments is the money we use to live the life we desire in retirement. Alternatively, many will focus first on the investment capital. They will focus on managing the capital to a specific degree of risk and focus on generating a specific amount of income. In the world of the traditional "capital centric" approach, the income is an outcome of the portfolio, rather than the portfolio being an outcome of the income. In this case, I am strongly advocating that the income strategy should drive the portfolio.

By focusing on the income first several outcomes occur:

- You will be able to determine the most tax-efficient way to receive income.
- You will be able to determine which sources of income to draw from first, second and third, so as to create the most tax-efficient income.
- You will be able to set some boundaries regarding the "risk profile" of the income. In other words, who wants to see their income fluctuate year over year or month over month? So, by focusing on the income first, several new rules appear to us.

Rule 1: Determine the most tax-efficient way to draw your income. To do so you must model your income on the tax return. This is something that should be done twice a year to ensure that you are drawing only the right amount of income from the right source at the right time so as to minimize tax.

Rule 2: Seek out the "lowest risk" income option. To do so, we need to set some boundaries on how to create a low risk income option. Rule 2 is about how the income is structured, rather than which products you use to achieve this outcome (see Rule 3).

Rule 3: Consider the 30% test. No more than 30% of your income should come from variable sources of income in retirement (such as an actively managed portfolio). The more you rely on the portfolio over time for success and the more income you draw from the portfolio each year, the greater the probability that you will run out of money prematurely in retirement.

Rule 4: Only draw the income you need, when you need it. Match the timing of your income with the timing of your expenses.

Rule 5: Always split income equally. The most efficient outcome for any retired couple is two equal incomes. In other words, one larger income and one smaller income often results in more taxes paid. If you have two equal incomes you may well pay less tax and have more money to spend each month.

However, to have two equal incomes in retirement, you need to plan ahead. You need to consider all sources of income available to each spouse and then save and invest in those areas that will help to balance out the income received in retirement. More on this in Chapter 5.

> *The tax return, when used wisely, is your greatest asset in retirement. Yet, if used unwisely, it can be your greatest enemy.*

Rule 6: Create multiple sources of income in retirement. This rule may not apply to everyone, depending on their income needs and their overall tax picture. If your family income in retirement is expected to exceed the Age Credit clawback level (see the appendix for more information) then creating additional savings in lower taxed investments is highly beneficial. Lower taxed investments would be Tax-Free Savings Accounts (TFSAs), dividends from a private company, investment products that pay out a "return of capital" and/or dividend income from a non-registered investment portfolio.

Principle 2: Be Clear on Your Expenses

There are always two sides to every story, and this is no different for retirement planning. On the one hand you need to generate enough income from your various income sources, but on the other hand you need to be mindful of how you are spending your money.

To use your money wisely in retirement, consider the following rules:

Rule 1: Focus on "after-tax" values (i.e.: your expenses). The only relevant figure when it comes to retirement income planning is the after-tax figure. Start from the ground up by focusing only on the "after-tax" values you need and want. In other words, the best way to make sure you are using your available income wisely is to spend just as much time tracking your expenses as you do focusing on your income.

Rule 2: Understand the timing of your expenses. As mentioned in the previous section, it is extremely beneficial to match the timing of your income with the timing of your expenses.

Rule 3: Differentiate between needs and wants. A "need" relates to your basic necessities whereas a "want" relates to your lifestyle choices. Typical needs include food, clothing, shelter, transportation and basic spending money. These are the typical "non-negotiables". Typical "lifestyle wants" include entertainment expenses (theatre tickets, hockey tickets), travel, and maintaining a family cottage or vacation home. The "wants" are those things that you could adjust over time as you so choose or as circumstances dictate. You may not want to make these adjustments, but nevertheless, they are adjustments you could make. This is also really important so as to understand your risks in retirement and the extent to which you have a "buffer".

By having a clear understanding of the types of expenses you incur, the timing of these expenses and the necessity of these expenses, you will begin to enjoy the freedom that comes from the after-tax income you receive. You see, when you have this type of clarity, your "values" begin to take over. You begin to make fewer "impulse" decisions and you make more "values based" decisions. You begin to know exactly what is important to you and what is not. That is when you begin to feel free with your money and the fun really begins.

So, to be a "Master" of your retirement, be clear about your income, but also be clear about your expenses. This leads us to Principle 3.

Principle 3: Something is only as Good as What You Compare it to

Every day each of us is faced with choices. Some choices are small and, regardless of the outcome, may have little impact on our lives. Alternatively, some choices are complex and may have a significant ripple effect into other areas. Some choices may have very little financial impact whereas others could have a significant financial impact.

However, regardless of the situation, when you evaluate a choice in isolation you may miss out on other important opportunities or you may create an unexpected negative financial outcome. In other words, something is only as good as what you compare it to, and therein lays the challenge.

You see, there are many great ideas, products and strategies to consider when planning your retirement, your retirement income, your health care needs and ultimately your final estate plan. If you were to look at each of these ideas, products or strategies on their own, you would easily conclude that all are great opportunities that you must act on today. Yet, a random collection of products or strategies can do just as much harm as good. How you "connect" multiple products and strategies will have just as much impact on your overall retirement success as the features or benefits of the product itself.

With this in mind, consider the following rules:

Rule 1: Know where you are today: What you have today is what we refer to as your "base line scenario".

Before considering any product, idea, concept or strategy, be clear as to where you stand today.

Rule 2: Always identify alternative choices: Never, ever look at a choice in isolation. Before proceeding with any investment product or strategy, always identify alternative choices. The first choice, of course, is whether you need to make any changes at all to your current approach. Referring back to Rule 1, if you don't know what your base line scenario is today, then how can you determine if it is broken or needs to be fixed? This simple step will help to keep you focused and help to protect you from making inappropriate decisions.

Rule 3: Consider the ripple effect: Very simply put, every "action" will have a corresponding "reaction". For example, to have more "guarantees" in retirement, you may have to accept lower returns, less income, higher fees or less liquidity (i.e.: less ability to sell when you want to). Before you proceed with any new investment or strategy, always consider the ripple effect. Ask yourself: "by making this change, is there a ripple effect that may violate or impact the Great Killers of Wealth and the Principles and Rules of Retirement Mastery outlined in this chapter?"

As the saying goes, "if you stand for nothing you will fall for anything". Unfortunately, due to the complexity of retirement in general, let alone the complexity of various investment products and the uncertainty of the current economic environment, it is easy to be persuaded emotionally to do things that may ultimately create more harm in the long term. To avoid this outcome, you must always compare the features, benefits and implications of various choices. You must focus on the details.

Principle 4: Assess Your Current Situation Annually

Your period of retirement could be as long as 20 or more years. Throughout this period things will change: your need for income, your investment values, your government benefits, your health, taxes and so on. Therefore, to create a retirement plan at the outset and then to never review your plan would be a considerable mistake.

With this in mind, it is important to consider the following issues each and every year:

Rule 1: Update your personal Net Worth Statement. Your personal Net Worth

Statement is a snapshot of everything you own and all the debts you owe. How has your net worth changed over the past year? Have your assets increased in value or decreased in value? Do the changes suggest that you can withdraw some capital, lend money to kids and grandkids or that you should tighten your belt? You see, if you don't know how things have changed over the previous year, then how can you ever feel confident when making any financial decision? Updating your personal Net Worth Statement annually and reviewing it with your advisor is extremely important to help you stay on track over time. We recommend that you update your Net Worth Statement every January.

Rule 2: Review your income and your expenses. As mentioned previously in this chapter, review the amount and timing of both income and expenses frequently each year as things will always change. To truly *Master Your Retirement* these details are extremely important. You always want to make sure you are on track, for both your income and your expenses, and if you are not, you are able to make changes quickly before the impact becomes significant.

Rule 3: Review the Great Killers of Wealth. Each year, consider the degree to which you have been successful in minimizing your taxes, investment management fees, the impact of inflation, the impact of long term interest costs and the impact of fluctuating investment markets. We recommend you consider this at least every January.

Rule 4: Review changes in government policy and programs. Each year the government will modify the tax brackets and the tax credit amounts, new programs may be launched and others may be eliminated. Since most of these programs impact the tax return (or are impacted by your tax return), it is important to stay on top of these changes. We recommend you do this every February, as this is the time when most of these announcements are made.

Specifically, since 2007, there have been significant changes to the tax return. These include the launch of the Pension Income Splitting rules, the launch of the Tax-Free Savings Account, continuous enhancements to the Registered Disability Savings Plan program, the enhancement of various credits (the age credit, pension income credit, disability credit, care giver credit, to name a few) as well as the continuous indexing of the tax brackets. The Provinces will also make similar changes within one to two years of the Federal tax changes, thus further enhancing the potential benefits available.

In the 2011 Federal Government Budget, further enhancements were made to the Guaranteed Income Supplement but increased restrictions were placed on new Individual Pension Plans for business owners.

It is important to review these types of changes annually and then to adapt your income withdrawal strategy to these changes. This will help to ensure that you always pay the least amount of tax over time while receiving the most amounts in government benefits.

Rule 5: Review the current environment. Are interest rates rising or falling? Is inflation rising more quickly or remaining steady and predictable? Is the stock market rising or is there increased volatility and risk since this time last year? Is the Canadian dollar rising or falling (as this may impact travel plans)? You see, by taking some time each year (or preferably three times a year, in May, October and December) to reflect on the current environment you are more able to react to changes in the world around you and/or adjust your portfolio pro-actively so as to protect your income and your capital.

Principle 5: Be Forward-Looking

To be successful in any activity, career or sport, one must always be "forward-looking". By this I mean that one must always look ahead to next year, to three years down the road or to a specific future scenario. Many scenarios in retirement are inevitable. At some point you will likely need increased health care assistance, you will likely need to change residences and you will pass away. In some instances, a surviving spouse may live alone for many, many years. In other situations, one spouse may be in a care home for many years while the other spouse remains in the original family home. To some degree or another, the scenarios are inevitable and so it is prudent to plan for them in advance.

Rule 1: Plan ahead for the next phase of retirement. Throughout this book I will discuss in more detail the Phases of Retirement. It is important to recognize that there are five phases that virtually all retirees will transition through in one way or another. With this in mind, it is important to acknowledge the phase that you are currently in today and the next phase that you may be entering. It is very important to consider the impact of each phase on your income, expenses, lifestyle and tax picture. This will help to avoid the impact of the Great Killers of Wealth and help you preserve your retirement plan over time.

Rule 2: Always have a Plan B. People will often get into trouble financially when they are either unable to adapt to these changing circumstances, or they fail to change their plan when the environment around them has clearly changed. In other words, if you expect the decisions you made last year to last indefinitely, I encourage you to think again. As the saying goes, the only constant over time is change. To be ready for this change, it is prudent to think ahead about how you would react should certain events occur. This is just good planning.

Rule 3: Think in terms of income and capital, in both life and in death. The key to long term financial success is to think about both your income and your capital, today and over the longer term.

It is also imperative to plan to maximize the benefits derived from your income and capital in both life (today, so that you can live the most gracious life possible) and in death (somewhere down the road). Planning ahead for the "final transition" of your income and capital to your heirs is one of the most significant financial events in your life. While it is easy to say that this final transition is not that important because, after all, you will be dead, it is an extremely important event because you have the ability now to determine how your hard earned wealth can play a role for the benefit of others for years and generations to come. Therefore, planning for this "final transition" in advance is another way in which you can make sure your wealth benefits those people and organizations most important to you.

IN SUMMARY

The Principles and Rules

If we were to take all of the principles and rules outlined in this chapter and boil it down to four words, those four words would be the following:

Accumulation – Growth – Preservation – Transition[1]

To truly *Master Your Retirement*, you begin with ensuring that you are receiving your income in the most efficient manner and in turn spending it in the manner that gives you the most security and joy. This is what we refer to as the "element of accumulation".

To truly *Master Your Retirement*, you will always strive to see your money grow over time. The rate of growth is best measured on the Net Worth Statement and ideally, growth is only what it needs to be, at as low a level of risk as possible. Yet, placing too much emphasis on growth may ultimately hurt you in the end. It is important, over time, to see growth in your income, so as to offset the effects of inflation, as well as growth in your investment capital and net worth. This is what we refer to as the "element of growth".

To truly *Master Your Retirement*, we must also focus on protecting both the income and capital you already have. If you know that both your income and your capital are safe, then you are free to live your life to its fullest joy and potential. This is what we refer to as the "element of preservation". The "element of growth" always needs to be tempered with the "element of preservation".

Finally, to truly *Master Your Retirement*, it is also important to think in terms of "transition". As mentioned at the end of this chapter, to maximize the tax-efficiency of income and capital, today and in death, we must be forward thinking. The reality is that income and capital that is shared between spouses will often pay considerably less tax than income and capital concentrated in the hands of just one spouse. Therefore, "transitioning" income and capital to others that are in lower income tax brackets must always be a consideration. We call this the "element of transition".

These are the four elements of a process we call RWM™ is designed to overcome the Great Killers of Wealth by following the Principles and Rules outlined in this chapter. Real Wealth Management is the key to fulfilling your dreams with peace of mind because it creates a discipline around making financial decisions.

---

[1] - Real Wealth Management™ is a strategic framework for making the best decisions to Accumulate, Grow, Preserve and Transition sustainable family wealth with the most purchasing power: after taxes, inflation and fees. Copyright to Knowledge Bureau, Inc.

Without this discipline, all you have are random decisions and random outcomes. Given how important your retirement period is, random outcomes are simply not an option. Predictable, reliable, low-risk options are the only acceptable approaches.

Things You Need to Know

- Develop the "Income Plan" first. Once you know where your income is likely to come from, you can then determine the most tax-efficient way to draw this income. This will then influence the investment of the portfolio and the degree of portfolio risk.

- Break down your expenses into meaningful categories. This will help you make important decisions as your income and expenses fluctuate over time.

- To measure progress, assess your current situation annually.

- To anticipate changes, or negative events, be forward-looking.

Questions You Need to Ask

- Is the income plan being developed first or is my income a result of what is generated by the portfolio?

- Am I following the rules outlined in this chapter?

- Does my retirement plan address the Great Killers of Wealth?

- What do I need to do to achieve greater efficiency, less tax and lower risk?

- Is my advisor able to help me with these things, or is he limited in what he can do because of his license?

Things You Need To Do

- Be aggressive. This is your retirement. Are things as efficient as they could be? What needs to be changed?

- Be thorough. Do you really know where your money is going and is this consistent with your values?

- Review frequently. By reviewing things frequently, you will be able to see small issues that can be easily corrected. If you do not review frequently, then you run the risk of falling off course and causing further hardship.

- Compare to other alternatives: something is only as good as what you compare it to.

- Display the "Principles" and "Rules" outlined in this chapter at the front of your retirement planning binder or on the wall in your home office.

Decisions You Need to Make

- Commit to the rules. Am I committed to following the rules outlined in this chapter? If not, why not?

Mastery Principle

Rules create discipline and predictable outcomes when applied consistently over time. Spend time to learn and implement the rules outlined in this chapter. Pay attention to the details and be forward-looking.

4

The Phases of Retirement

"The most splendid achievement of all is the constant striving to surpass yourself and to be worthy of your own approval." DENIS WAITLEY

Cal and Marnie had dinner the other night with three other couples. Each of the couples is about the same age, but when it comes to retirement, they are all at different stages. Cal and Marnie retired last fall. Even though they are now retired, they are still uncertain as to how much money they will need and how they will spend their time. Cal and Marnie looked forward to their retirement, but they feel like they have been "holding back" and they are not sure why.

Bill and Rhonda have been retired for close to 10 years now; they have been travelling extensively, enjoying their grandchildren and spending considerable time at the lake during the summer. The recent downturn in the equity markets, however, has caused a dent in their typical yearly plans. In the first few years of retirement they were able to be away for months at a time, now they feel they can only afford to go on smaller trips that are also closer to home. They are concerned about their money and their lifestyle and are unsure of what the future holds. They wish they could have more certainty in their life by getting back the capital that was lost.

Rick and Bonnie have been semi-retired for six years but have been less fortunate. Rick had to retire for medical reasons and the medical expenses continue to be considerable. Bonnie continued to work full-time for the past five years and is now beginning to drop her hours down to part time. Their vision of retirement is certainly not panning out as planned. They are concerned about Rick's health and are looking for ways to optimize their income and reduce their taxes. They are unsure of how to address these issues.

Stan and Jessie are just not interested in retiring as of yet. They are partners in a small business that, while challenging at times, has continued to grow and has been a great source of income and enjoyment. They continue to talk about retiring in the next couple of years but they have been saying that forever. Why they haven't retired may be a mystery to those looking in from the outside. Stan and Jessie have been excellent savers, but they are unsure of the best way to draw from their savings. They would like to continue to operate the business for as long as they can, but they are unsure if they should continue to draw a salary, pay a dividend, draw from their RRSPs or all of the above.

THE ISSUES

Each of these couples is in the same age range, but is living through very different circumstances.

Cal and Marnie are struggling to figure out how much money they will actually need in retirement, even though they have already been fully retired for a year.

Bill and Rhonda are struggling to figure out how to recover some of the investments they lost during the market downturn.

Rick and Bonnie are consumed with medical issues and medical expenses. They want to make sure they are receiving all of the tax benefits available so that their lifestyle remains intact and so that Bonnie can fully retire one day.

Stan and Jessie are most concerned with how they will draw their income in retirement. They have several sources from which to draw, but they are not sure what to do first, second or third.

Each of these situations is very real. Hundreds of thousands of Canadian couples are facing similar issues in their retirement plans. We recognize from this that even though these couples are of similar age, they are actually in different "phases" of retirement. Each phase has common features with the other, but there are also unique considerations in each.

There are five different phases of retirement through which literally every individual will pass. In some cases, one or more phase may last a period of days or weeks while other phases may last many years. Each phase brings with it a unique set of challenges that must be adhered to or you run the risk of falling off course. Therefore, in each phase we must consider the Killers of Wealth as well as the Rules of Mastery to ensure we stay on course.

Phase 1: The Pre-Retirement Years

This is typically the 7 to 10 years before you are completely finished working. You may work part time during this phase so as to gradually transition to full time retirement living. For some this period may be between the ages of 45 and 55, while for others it may be between the ages of 70 and 75. The difference in the ages may have nothing to do with money. Rather, it may have everything to do with lifestyle desires and the personal satisfaction that comes from work. When it comes to retirement there is no right or wrong and the answers to your questions may not be black and white. Rather, the right answers for you are based on your own personal preferences and comfort zone. Continue to do whatever you enjoy and do your best to avoid the "stereotypes" that suggest what you should or should not be doing at this stage in life.

This is the phase that Stan and Jessie are in today.

Phase 2: The First Two Years

The first two years of full retirement is often a period of significant adjustment. During this time you will gain a better understanding of your basic income needs as well as your lifestyle wants. In the previous phase you created some projections of what you were expecting to happen. Now you are able to compare your projections with real life experiences. You will also begin to forge a new routine. The relationship between you and your spouse may evolve significantly during this time or you may find yourself going through one of those rough patches. You will begin to sort out activities you wish to do on your own and those you wish to do together. You will spend more time with others who are of a similar age and doing the same types of activities. You may do things that you never thought you'd do.

In this phase it is tempting for many to make some big decisions, the most common of which has to do with your home. Be patient during this time and do not make any significant decisions. The First Two Years is time for adjustment, trial and error and reflection. What you "thought" you may want to do in retirement may very well change during these first two years. The people you thought you'd spend time with may also change. It is prudent to resist the temptation to rush into any big decisions. This is a time to try as many different things as possible.

At this stage many answers have been found to the questions you had just a few years ago. However, there are still more questions that may have come to the fore. You may be confirming your original plans and you may be writing, changing and updating these original plans. Much will change in the first two years of retirement so "let the dust settle" and try not to make any big decisions at this time unless absolutely necessary (usually related to a specific health issue).

Cal and Marnie are in this phase today.

Phase 3: The Active Years

The retired individual or couple often has the greatest clarity and drive during this phase. People are clear as to what they wish to do, where they wish to go, and with whom they wish to spend time. During this time the couple is very active, often more active and busy than during the working years. They are very focused, determined and purposeful in how they spend their time. In many situations the couple shares a sense of urgency for certain priorities. Friends, family, spouse are active, healthy and vibrant. For some this may be a period of time that lasts 10 to 15 years while for others, as luck would have it, may be only a time of one to two years. When planning this stage it is important to keep in mind the age of your children and grandchildren. You can easily project the ages and life activities of your loved ones around you and, with this information in mind, you can plan your own active lifestyle with confidence and enthusiasm.

With this in mind, it is important to recognize that some couples never get out of Phase 2 and into Phase 3. By this I mean that they live the first two years of retirement over and over again. They are never certain as to their financial situation and they are never totally sure of how they wish to spend their time. Needless to say, this is quite tragic as they will never be able to fully enjoy all that life has to offer.

Bill and Rhonda are in Phase 3 today.

Phase 4: When Illness Strikes

As we age it is hard not to notice changes in our bodies and our minds. New aches and pains begin to set in making it more and more difficult to do the things you most wish to do. In more serious situations the illness requires invasive surgery, perhaps months of hospital treatments and/or a new regimen of daily medications. This phase will inevitably transition one spouse to the role of caregiver, adding considerable fatigue and financial hardship on the healthy spouse, especially if the final diagnosis is a long term debilitating disease. Watching your lifelong friend, lover and partner go through such an illness can be extremely agonizing and stressful. This stress may also transition to the extended family. One day you may even find that the "healthy" spouse is just not able to keep up with the needs of the spouse with the illness. At this time the discussion takes place of moving one, or both of you, to a more suitable housing facility. This is a period in time that could last months or as long as a decade.

Even though Bonnie is still working, she and Rick are in this phase.

Phase 5: When You are on Your Own Again

A final phase of retirement for many is the time spent on their own after the death of their spouse. For some this may be a period of 10 to 20 years, while for others it may be a matter of months. Regardless of the situation the surviving spouse may now be in charge of certain areas of his or her life that he or she has never had to deal with in the past. A common example of this is the finances. If the individual who handled the finances of the household is the one who passes away first, the surviving spouse can often find these new responsibilities to be very intimidating. The decisions that need to be made after the death of a spouse can be daunting, while the decisions regarding the final transition of your assets to your beneficiaries may create even more stress, fatigue and insecurity.

This is something that faces all four couples. None of these couples have reached this phase as of yet, but it could be a phase that arrives at any time. All four couples are thinking about this and they all wish to prepare for it accordingly.

Within each of these phases, there are also three to five year periods of time that also require your attention. As mentioned in chapter 1, there will be periods when you wish to focus your time and attention on particular activities. During the Active Years, for example, there may be periods of time when you travel extensively and there may be periods of time when you focus on volunteer activities in your home city. Remember, life is a journey of cumulative experiences and activities.

THE SOLUTIONS

The Phases of Retirement teach us many things. First, to address any specific issue or challenge, it is helpful to break down this challenge into smaller pieces. We recognize throughout this book that retirement is complex and the best way to break through this complexity is to break things down into meaningful pieces.

The common pieces that fit all four couples relate back to the Killers of Wealth and the Principles and Rules discussed in the last two chapters. Specifically, all four couples are impacted by taxes, fees, inflation, borrowing costs and market volatility. The extent to which they can reduce taxes and fees, the more money they will have to protect or enhance their lifestyle. They can all benefit by following each of the Principles and the Rules:

Focus on Income First, Then Capital

You can see how the "income" question impacts each of the couples regardless of the phase of retirement. Even for Bill and Rhonda, who are looking for ways to recover the capital they have lost, focusing on "income first" is still the best way to address this issue. All of life's benefits begin with the income, which will ultimately influence the design and risk profile of the investment portfolio.

Each of the couples is interested in receiving the most amount of income while paying the least amount of tax (Rule 1). After-all, who wouldn't want this? Yet, each situation is slightly different because of the different types of income they have. Cal and Marnie have mostly pension income while Stan and Jessie have mostly RRSP and dividend income from their savings inside their company. Bill and Rhonda have mostly investment income while Rick and Bonnie are looking for ways to maximize tax deductions against this income. Between the four couples there could easily be close to 25 different sources of income. Some sources will be available today while others may not be available until they each turn 65 (i.e.: Old Age Security). Some sources of income they will draw from today while other sources they may not draw from until age 71 (i.e.: RRSPs). Some sources of income they may draw from today but, in the future, they may draw less income or no income from them (i.e.: from a TFSA). As you move from one phase to another your sources of income will change.

Bill and Rhonda are learning the hard way in terms of what it means to "seek out the lowest risk income option" (Rule 2). Most of their income was coming from their actively managed investment portfolio. During years when the markets were rising, they would draw out the income they need and still see the value of their portfolio grow from year to year. Yet, when the 2008 market downturn hit, the market decline combined with the withdrawals for the year to put the portfolio down to a level not seen in a decade. Unfortunately, Bill and Rhonda did not realize that their income and portfolio was as high a risk as what it turned out to be.

Alternatively, when Rick and Bonnie structured their retirement income, they stuck to the boundaries of the 30% test (Rule 3). Rick and Bonnie wanted to make sure that no more than 30% of their income would come from their actively managed investment portfolio. By following this discipline, when the 2008 downturn occurred, 30% of their income declined by only 15%. In other words, their income declined by only 4.5% on a before-tax basis (30% X 15% = 4.5%). On an after-tax basis, their income declined by even less. To calculate the 30% test, Rick and Bonnie considered all of their various income sources and thus had the option of taking Rick's pension income as is, transferring the value of Rick's pension to a locked-in retirement account or transferring the value of Rick's pension to a life insurance company to purchase an annuity. Rick and Bonnie ended up transferring most of the pension to an annuity and kept the balance in an actively managed investment account. It's a good thing they did this because, as things turned out, if their portfolio had fallen in value at a time when Rick's health care costs had gone up, the result would have been disastrous.

Be Clear on Your Expenses

Regardless of the phase, you must always be aware of where your money is going. This is the only way in which you will be able to make meaningful changes to your life over time. However, we can see that the expenses you will incur will be different depending on the phase of retirement you enjoy. In some cases the expenses will be more focused on lifestyle and/or trying out different activities whereas in other phases the expenses may be more focused on medical issues.

Bill and Rhonda, for the first several years of retirement, were most concerned with the gross, before tax rate of return on their investments. They clearly stated to their investment advisor that they needed to have an 8% return on their investment portfolio. What Bill and Rhonda didn't realize is that a portfolio with an 8% rate of return meant that they were taking a considerable amount of risk and that a correction of 20% or more would be very normal for this type of investment return. Bill and Rhonda also didn't realize that there were ways in which they could draw their income more "tax-efficiently" meaning that they didn't need to take as much risk. Now they realize that the best way to start their planning is by clearly identifying their "after-tax income amounts" (Rule 1). By first determining what they really needed for after-tax income, they were then able to work this backwards to determine how to achieve this income in the most tax-efficient and low risk manner. When they understood the amount and type of income they needed from their portfolio, they could then have the portfolio designed to produce this outcome in the lowest risk manner. Bill and Rhonda learned from this experience that the best way to achieve their objectives is to be clear about what their expenses are from an after-tax point of view.

Cal and Marnie have spent their first 12 months of retirement tracking all of their expenses and comparing them with the budgets they prepared prior to retirement. They were curious to see how close real life was to their expectations. Like most couples, Cal and Marnie realized that there are more ways to spend the money than they had originally anticipated. While this was stressful at first, they both began to realize that their spending habits were a great reflection of their own values. This helped them to easily "differentiate between their needs and their wants" (Rule 3). Now, whenever a new opportunity presents itself, they are easily able to determine where this opportunity fits within their values and when it trumps any of their other "wants". Cal and Marnie are becoming more and more focused on those activities and events that give them the most joy and satisfaction, all because they began to differentiate between their "needs" and their "wants".

Something is Only as Good as What You Compare it to

All of these couples have choices; however, the choices they have are related to their phase of retirement.

Stan and Jessie, in Phase 1, are choosing between different combinations of income sources and whether to retire now, in a few years' time or gradually over a longer period of time. Stan and Jessie will compare the pros and cons of retiring now versus later as it relates to the lifestyle that is most important to them today and in the future. For Stan and Jessie to effectively choose between retiring now or later, they must first be clear as to "where they are today" (Rule 1). To understand where they are today they must know things such as: i) what are all of their available income sources; ii) how much income would come from each source; iii) how each source would be taxed; iv) how much after-tax income would remain, and v) how this after-tax income amount compares to their current income needs. By having a clear understanding of where they are today, they can then compare this scenario to any other alternative scenario so as to determine the best overall approach, for them, today.

Cal and Marnie, in Phase 2, are choosing between different types of retirement activities. They have tried out different things and are looking to see what sticks. They too will be looking at different combinations of income so as to achieve the most benefit and clearly see what lifestyle options are available to them over time. They may also be choosing between staying in their current home or moving to a condo, living at the lake or spending more time down south. To make this decision, it is helpful for Cal and Marnie to consider the pros and cons of different choices, before they act on any one specific choice. It is important to recognize that any time Cal and Marnie sell or buy a property, they are dealing with legal fees, land transfer taxes and realty fees. These fees can easily add up to over $20,000 for each transaction. If Cal and Marnie were to make a quick decision and decide to buy or sell a property, and then find out shortly after that they would have preferred another option, they may find that they have incurred $20,000 to $60,000 in fees and commissions over a very short period of time. This is a waste of their hard earned wealth. Therefore, before making any significant life decision, always consider the pros and cons of your choice and take all the time necessary to think it through before acting (Rule 2). This is the "element of preservation"- protecting what you have already built.

In all of these situations there is also a "ripple effect" (Rule 3). Sir Isaac Newton's third law of motion stated: "Forces always occur in pairs. Every action is accompanied by a reaction of equal magnitude." The same is true with all things financial. Every financial decision has a corresponding reaction that hopefully is positive, but has an equal chance of being negative. Therefore, financial decisions, particularly in retirement, should never be taken lightly or quickly. After any decision is made, there is a "ripple effect". Before making any decision it is important to consider i) what this ripple effect may be, ii) the degree to which it may be positive or negative, and iii) in the event that it is negative, how you will respond.

Assess Your Current Situation Annually

All four couples are assessing their current situation, but unless this assessment is broken down into meaningful pieces will they be able to fully understand their choices? In other words, most problems can seem daunting and overwhelming. Therefore, to address any problem you must first break the problem down into smaller pieces.

All four couples have been good at taking some time to review the current economic and investment environment (Rule 5). Cal and Marnie are wondering if today is a good day to be selling their real estate. Bill and Rhonda are wondering what is next for the stock market. Rick and Bonnie are wondering about the impacts of not only inflation but of health care inflation in particular. Stan and Jessie are wondering about the economy and whether they can expect to see their business continue to grow in a strong economy or whether it will be impacted by an inevitable recession. While it is always difficult to know for sure what the future holds, simply by taking a little amount of time every three to six months to assess the state of the current economic and investment environment (we recommend three times a year), you will be able to see the trends as they ebb and flow over time. This is extremely important because if Cal and Marnie could wait one or two more years to sell their home, they may end up with many thousands of dollars of additional equity. If Bill and Rhonda put all their hopes into a rising stock market, they may be disappointed and financially hurt if this does not happen right away. Rick and Bonnie, if they don't plan ahead, may find that their purchasing power declines significantly over time. Stan and Jessie may miss an ideal opportunity to sell their business.

At all stages in retirement, assessing your situation annually is the best way to protect yourself from an unexpected, yet identifiable economic calamity or significant life event. This is extremely important because you have literally only one chance to get it right in retirement. You don't want to be that person, or that couple, that has to go back to work because their retirement was "priced to perfection" and the life events were anything but perfect. In some instances, consumers will elect to use investment products that provide some form of guarantee or are simply just of lower risk. Yet, if the cost of the guarantee and/or the tax paid on this lower risk investment (i.e.: GIC interest for example) is to the tune of several thousand dollars a year, you can be much further ahead by simply paying attention to the rules mentioned above at all phases of retirement.

There is just no substitute for taking the time to be involved with your own money.

Be Forward-Looking

Once you have taken the time to be on top of your current situation, it is also important to be forward-looking.

As mentioned previously, each of the Phases of Retirement can last only a handful of days or be as long as a decade. Therefore, it is prudent to take some time each year to consider the impact that the next phase of retirement may have on your overall retirement plan (Rule 1). You will want to consider the changes in your income and expenses, taxes and the availability of government benefits.

When you look back on your life, you can always see that things have not always turned out as planned. How you recovered from these circumstances will have likely had a huge impact on where you are today. Therefore, by always "having a Plan B" (Rule 2), you will be able to protect yourself from significant negative events such as an unexpected death of a spouse, ailing health, rising interest rates, rising inflation, rising taxes and falling stock markets. All four couples need to ask questions like: what would happen if my spouse became ill or passed away? How would this impact my life and my finances? How would rising interest rates, rising inflation, rising taxes or falling stock markets impact my income, expenses and lifestyle choices? By focusing on these types of questions, several outcomes occur:

- While the arrival of the event itself may be a shock, your response will be measured and prepared. You will already know what you are going to do.
- You are able to adapt quickly to minimize the impact.
- You are able to remain focused on the "life issues" because your "financial issues" will have been already addressed.

Remember, this is all about "Mastering Your Retirement". This is all about Fulfilling Your Dreams with Peace of Mind. By having a Plan B in place, both you and your spouse will be well prepared for anything that may come your way. This gives you the confidence and peace of mind to deal with any circumstance that will arrive, regardless of the phase of retirement you are in today, and the phase you are moving toward in the future.

The best way to Master Your Retirement is to follow the Rules in each of the Phases of Retirement.

When you look back at your life, you will also see that it is made up of a series of transitions: from school to work, from one type of job to another, from one type of home to another, from various degrees of health and wellness to changes in your relationships. To say the least, your life up to now has been a constant evolution. With this in mind, it is obvious to see that your life going forward will be very much the same: a series of transitions. We have discussed at length in this chapter that there are Phases of Retirement, which will ultimately be seen over time as a series of transitions from one phase to another. Knowing this, we can use this information to our advantage when it comes to finances: Be Forward-Looking: Transition both your income and capital in life and in death (Rule 3).

IN SUMMARY

The Phases of Retirement

In this chapter we have discussed the Phases of Retirement. With this information, we hope you recognize that how you prepare for each phase can either positively or negatively impact your life experience during each phase. Each phase is unique, having its own unique issues. Yet, the Killers of Wealth are with us at all times and must be addressed by following the Rules of Mastery.

Things You Need To Know

- Success is not a random event. Success comes from preparation and avoiding large, unexpected losses.
- The age you are at does not necessarily mean that you will be at a certain phase in retirement. Four couples, each the same age, could be at four different phases of retirement.
- You can get stuck in any one of the phases and never move beyond it. This is not healthy and you should be exploring why this is happening.

Questions You Need To Ask

- What phase am I in today?
- What phase am I moving into next?
- What are the issues that could cause hardship to me in the next phase?
- What do we need to do to prepare for the next phase?

Things You Need To Do

- Understand the unique issues and characteristics of each phase.
- Look around you at other retired couples and identify the phase they are likely in today.

- Observe the issues they are dealing with and consider ways in which you would deal with the same situation if or when it arises for you.

Decisions You Need To Make

- Commit to identifying your current Phase of Retirement.
- Commit to identifying the most important risks and opportunities to you in this phase.
- Commit to identifying the most important risks and opportunities to you in your next Phase of Retirement.
- Commit to resolving these issues in advance so that when this transition takes place, you and your spouse are ready.

Mastery Principle

Be prepared. Things change when you least expect it. How you will react and how you will be impacted has everything to do with how well you are prepared. Prepare a buffer to your plan.

5

Seven to Ten Years Before Retirement

"Each day is a miraculous gift; our job
is to untie the ribbons." GREG ANDERSON

Natalie and Nate are in their late 40s. Their oldest child started university this year and they expect that their youngest will be finished university in about six years' time. At this stage in their life, their focus has begun to shift toward their life after kids.

- *How much longer will they work?*
- *How much more do they need to save for retirement?*
- *Are they saving in the right types of investments?*
- *Are they taking the right amount of risk?*
- *What other sources of income will they have in their retirement?*

Natalie and Nate feel that they may retire seven to 10 years from now. They have been saving all they can up to now but really haven't paid that much attention to their investments. Now things are becoming that much more important and urgent to them.

How do they proceed from here?

THE ISSUES

The first of the five phases of retirement is "the pre-retirement years". In this edition of the *Master Your Retirement* book, I will break down this phase into two parts: i) the pre-retirement period that is seven to ten years prior to retirement (in this chapter), and ii) the period that is two years prior to retirement (in the next chapter).

At this stage of life it is natural for couples to begin to ask if they are "on track" to meeting their retirement goals and to determine a realistic retirement date. In most cases, these are financial issues. To calculate the answer to these questions, many "retirement planning software tools" will perform a long term retirement income calculation. The calculation will begin by asking for the amount of pre-tax income you are likely to need by a specific date. For most people, this is a hard question to answer because there are so many variables to consider. As a result, the "default" is to assume that you would need approximately 70% of your pre-tax retirement income at that time. In this example, let's assume that the pre-retirement income was $100,000 and that in 10 years' time the retirement income objective is $70,000 before tax. The software would then take this income amount and index it for inflation over the next 20 to 30 years of retirement. Assuming a 3% rate of inflation, over a 25 year period of time, a $70,000 pre-tax income at that time would need to be $146,564 of income at age 80 to 85 so as to maintain the purchasing power of what we know $70,000 provides today. This is the long term effect of inflation and is very real. The software will then work these figures back to today to determine what needs to be saved each year so that there is enough money to meet this long term income need.

In many cases, the monthly savings amount is significantly higher than what the family could afford to do today. This would then suggest that the retirement date needs to be postponed, the savings amount needs to be increased or their rate of return needs to be higher.

In my view, I believe that these types of calculations run the risk of over shooting the real need for savings because many of these programs focus on before tax income rather than after-tax income. I also believe that these types of programs can encourage unnecessary risk taking by suggesting a long term average return of 8% (for example) would help you achieve your investment return vs. the 7% long term average return used in the illustration. On the surface, the difference between an 8% return and a 7% return does not appear to be that significant to either the client or the advisor, yet it is. As people approach retirement and find they have not achieved their average return of 8%, they will often encourage the advisor to take more risk so as to achieve a higher return. This approach will ultimately end up with a bad outcome should the client see a negative return on their investments one to three years prior to their planned retirement date.

So what's the answer? What is a better way to determine if one is on track? What is a better way to determine the right amount to save? What is a better way to achieve the retirement goals while taking less risk in the portfolio?

THE SOLUTIONS

We call the seven to ten year period prior to retirement the "Tactical Saving Period". This is the stage of life when you want to do more than just sock some money away. "Where" you invest this money is extremely important. This emphasizes the importance of combining the principle of being forward-looking with the principle of being detail oriented.

We will begin with the end in mind: the tax return…in retirement. Depending on when you retire and the types of income available at that time, your tax position could be at one extreme or another.

For example, let's look at two couples. Couple A has $500,000 of RRSP savings, all of which is in the husband's name and couple B has $500,000 of non-registered investments that are jointly owned between the spouses. Each couple receives a combined total of $1200 per month in CPP income.

Tax Picture: Couple A

	Husband	Wife	Total
RRSP	$25,000.00		$25,000.00
CPP	$7,200.00	$7,200.00	$14,400.00
Dividends			$ –
Total	$32,200.00	$7,200.00	$39,400.00
Tax	$3,799.28		$3,799.28
Net	$28,400.72	$7,200.00	$35,600.72

Couple A would pay approximately $3,800 in taxes each year. If this remained the same for the next 25 years, couple A would pay total income tax of about $95,000 over their retirement years.

Tax Picture: Couple B

Receiving dividend income from their non-registered investments.

	Husband	Wife	Total
RRSP			$ –
CPP	$7,200.00	$7,200.00	$14,400.00
Dividends	$12,500.00	$12,500.00	$25,000.00
Total	$19,700.00	$19,700.00	$39,400.00
Tax			
Net	$19,700.00	$19,700.00	$39,400.00

Couple B would pay no tax on this income.

Note: These are very generic tax calculations that will vary based on the year, province and age of the individuals involved, but the concept remains the same.

By comparison, if couple B invested their non-registered money into GICs, for example, their tax picture would be the same as Couple A.

In other words, the type and amount of income you receive has
everything to do with the tax outcome.

Based on the amount and type of income received by Couple A, they may NOT have enough income to retire. However, couple B may have more than enough to retire simply by the fact that they have different types of investments that are taxed differently. This goes back to our "Rules": always focus on the amount of "after-tax income" required rather than the "before tax income" required. This clearly suggests to me that all "retirement planning software packages" must focus on the after-tax needs and wants of individuals rather than on the before tax needs and wants. By focusing on the after-tax needs and wants, you can then work it back to where you are today to determine how much you should save in the RRSP, the TFSA or any other investment product.

Ok, so what if Nate and Natalie were Couple A today. Where should they save and invest going forward to end up with the best outcome on their tax return in retirement?

What if there were three different saving options available to Nate and Natalie? What if each of these scenarios produced very different tax outcomes? Depending on how they save, what if they could end up paying $6,017 a year in tax (scenario 1), $5,297 a year in tax (scenario 2) or $4,355 a year in tax (scenario 3)? Obviously, the less tax you pay, the more income you will have available to spend

Over 25 years of retirement, the differences are significant:

- $42,000 in fewer taxes paid (in scenario 3 vs. scenario 1).
- $20,691 in additional after-tax income received (in scenario 3 vs. scenario 1).

Needless to say, these are significant figures. This only goes to show that paying attention to the details can really add up. Paying attention to where you save can make all the difference in the world. In many situations these figures can be five to 10 times higher. In other words, by changing around the amounts invested into different areas and thus changing the tax implications, many situations result in a difference of anywhere from $150,000 to $300,000 in additional after-tax income received.

Now, what if scenario 1, for example, could be enhanced further if Nate and Natalie took the refund from their RRSP contributions and reinvested it back into the RRSP or TFSA?. Or, what if scenario 3 could be enhanced if the savings amounts were invested into the TFSA rather than a fully taxable investment account? In this latter scenario you would have been able to reduce taxes paid by another 10%. Again, this is significant. Now we are up to reducing taxes by close to $50,000.

I have hopefully demonstrated to you that "where you invest and the amount you invest is extremely important". In my view, the only way to really answer Nate and Natalie's question is to project forward multiple scenarios and then model those scenarios on the tax return. Where you save your money is actually more important than the amount you save. Going back to the earlier conversation about using long term retirement planning software to answer these questions, you can begin to see that most software is focused on determining "the amount to save" rather than "where to save". By doing so, you can see that in some situations you run the risk of over-calculating the amount of money that actually needs to be saved. These calculations may also result in a game plan that pays way too much tax and recommends to the investor that they take on considerably more risk with their investment portfolio.

As a result, the focus must be on the tax return. To ignore tax is to ignore the most fundamental component of your retirement plan. Tax could mean the difference between "having enough" and "not having enough".

Tax is life's single greatest expense and the greatest Killer of Wealth.

Using the Tax Return as Your Guide

Ok, so what rules should we follow when evaluating outcomes using the tax return? There are several rules to consider at all times:

1. The Tax Return Changes at Age 60, 65 and 72 for Most Individuals in Retirement

The tax return changes at age 60 because you may potentially begin to draw your Canada Pension Plan retirement benefit at that time. This may mean more total income which may mean higher total taxes, unless you change how you draw your income. Age 65 is the time when most people, over the next 10 years, begin to receive Old Age Security (Note, if you turn 65 later than 2023, you may not receive the Old Age Security benefit until you turn age 67). Again, this may change the amount of income received and the tax paid on this income. Old Age Security begins to be clawed back when your individual income begins to exceed a specific level, which is indexed with inflation and thus changes every year (see the technical appendix for more information). Does your total income begin to exceed the OAS clawback level due to the fact that you are now receiving Old Age Security? If so, the extent to which you can "rebalance" your income sources at that time will help to reduce your taxes. Also, at age 65 the Age Credit begins to take effect. Once your taxable income begins to exceed a specific level, which is indexed with inflation and thus changes every year (see the technical appendix for more information) then you begin to lose the credit you received on your income up to this point. Therefore, the type of income you receive above the Age Credit clawback level will have a significant impact on the tax you pay below this same level. Finally, age 71 is when you must convert your remaining RRSPs to a RRIF, which means another source of income could begin in the year you turn 72. Therefore, as a simple rule of thumb, project your values forward to ages 60, 65 and 72 and measure the impact on the tax return.

2. Watch Your Tax Bracket

Your income is taxed based on a combination of Federal and Provincial tax. The amount of tax you pay on the next dollar of income rises the more money you earn.

For example, below are the marginal tax rates for Manitoba for different types of income for 2014. These are the combined Federal and Provincial Tax Rates:

Tax Bracket	Income	Capital Gains	Public Co. Dividends	CCPC Dividends
First $31,000	25.80%	12.90%	3.84%	16.46%
$31,000 - $43,953	27.75%	13.88%	6.53%	18.77%
$43,953 - $67,000	34.75%	17.38%	16.19%	27.03%
$67,000 - $87,907	39.40%	19.70%	22.6%	32.51%
$87,907 - $136,270	43.40%	21.70%	28.12%	37.23%
$136,270+	46.40%	23.20%	32.26%	40.77%

Source: www.taxtips.ca/taxrates/mb

The tax bracket refers to the amount of income earned. For example, on the first $31,000 of income earned the tax rate is 25.80%, but the tax rate on the income earned between $31,000 and $43,953 is 27.75%. "Income" refers to RRSP withdrawals, RRIF income, salary income, rental income, interest income and pension income.

A capital gain is the tax rate paid on the growth of "taxable" investments. If you own a stock in a taxable investment account, and that stock grows from $100 to $200, the capital gain is the difference between the price you sold the stock for and the price you paid for it. In this case, the capital gain is $100; 50% of this gain is then taxable as income, which is why you see, in the table above, that the tax rate on capital gains is 50% of the tax paid on "income" (because only 50% of the gain is taxable).

Dividends received from public companies, such as the Royal Bank, in a taxable investment account, are "grossed-up" and then a "tax credit" is applied against the grossed up amount. The net difference is then taxed as income. In the end, the net tax rate is shown above. Note how the tax rate on public company dividends is very low until you get up to $43,000 in income. Also note how the tax rate on public dividends is significantly less than the tax paid on income when you get to the higher income levels. If, for example, you had interest income that was being taxed at 34.75%, you could change this interest income to dividend income so that the tax on this income would drop down to 16.19%. If you were receiving $20,000 in interest income from GICs, for example, the tax paid would be approximately $6,950. Yet, if you received the same income from dividends the tax paid would be only $3,238. This simple change results in a potential tax saving of $3712 each and every year you are retired. Over 25 years, this is a difference of $92,800. You will potentially receive $92,800 more income throughout your retirement just by changing how this income is taxed.

Canadian Controlled Private Corporation (CCPC) dividends are those paid from a privately controlled enterprise. Many entrepreneurs will have money saved inside of their corporations. They may choose to pay out this income as a dividend. Note the difference in the tax rate between the taxes on CCPC dividends when compared with other options. In many cases the total tax paid may be the same when you compare the corporate tax paid plus the tax paid on the CCPC dividend to the tax on salary income. However, every situation is unique and there are many advantages to entrepreneurs using CCPC dividends as a source of income in retirement.

What does this teach us?

- As you layer on more and more income in retirement, the tax on that income increases.

- Different types of income are taxed at different rates.

- Having multiple sources of income to choose from in retirement is extremely important.

- Choosing when to draw from each source is an important way to manage your taxes (and defeat this mighty Killer of Wealth).

3. Take Full Advantage of the Basic Personal Amount[2]

Every taxpayer has a "basic personal amount" available. There is an amount for Federal Tax and an amount for the Provincial Tax, which is unique to each province. This means that you don't pay any Federal tax until your income exceeds

---

[2] see appendix

the Federal Amount and you won't begin to pay Provincial Tax until your income exceeds the Provincial amount. It is important that you are aware of your basic personal amount for the province in which you reside. The amount is important because you want to make sure that each eligible taxpayer has at least this much income to their name each and every year. This is one simple way to manage and reduce your taxes. The basic amounts are illustrated in the Technical Appendix.

4. Watch the Clawback Zones

There are two key clawback zones to watch for: i) the Age Credit Clawback and ii) the Old Age Security Clawback (See the Technical Appendix for more details). Both of these benefits become available at age 65. The ideal objective is to i) have all taxable income be less than the OAS clawback amount per spouse each year and ii) have lower taxed income sources above the Age Credit clawback level rather than higher taxed income sources.

By using these four basic parameters as a way to "evaluate" the tax return outcomes at age 60, 65 and 72, you begin to see some interesting results:

- You begin to see if you should ideally have more or less income from certain sources at each age.
- You begin to see where you should save from this point forward.
- You begin to see which source of income you should ideally draw from first, second and third.
- You begin to see that there are three key tax zones to pay attention to at age 65 and older: Tax Zone 1: The Basic Amount Up to the Age Amount Clawback Level, Tax Zone 2: The Age Amount Clawback level up to the OAS Clawback level and Tax Zone 3: Income above the OAS Clawback level. These three tax zones act as a guide to help determine which source of income should be drawn at each age.
- Finally, you begin to see how this money should be invested to achieve these results.

This approach is very different than what you will find with most retirement planning software packages. Most software tools will not necessarily optimize the income so as to pay the least amount of tax and most software will not necessarily optimize the income sources so as to "save the least amount" to get the greatest after-tax income. This is why you can often get very different "retirement plans" when following these two different retirement planning approaches.

Over the past 20 years I have used both approaches and my conclusion is that the most effective and simplest approach is the one I am advocating in this chapter and throughout this book.

Where You Save is More Important than the Amount You Save

There are three aspects to "where" you save:

- The type of product category (RRSP, TFSA, taxable investment account).
- Who actually invests this money (spouse A or B)?
- The type of investment product selected (stocks, bonds, GICs, ETFs or mutual funds).

In the remaining sections of this chapter I will discuss each of these three areas.

Understanding Product Types

The following concept is something we call the "Order of Investing". Since "tax" is life's single greatest expense, when we add a "tax overlay" to the decision of where to invest we discover some interesting outcomes.

We begin with the understanding that there are several specific investment choices. You could put your hard earned money into any number of different options:

- RRSPs, Spousal RRSPs, Pension Plan investments.
- Tax-Free Savings Accounts.
- Registered Education Savings Plan.
- Taxable Investment Accounts.
- Your Principle Residence.
- Rental Property.
- Vacation Property.
- Leveraged Investment Loans.

In the spirit of our "Rules", since something is only as good as what you compare it to, let's see how each of these investments compares from a "tax" point of view.

For each of these investment types, we need to look at the tax from three perspectives: i) the tax paid before you make this investment, ii) the tax paid as the investment grows/as distributions are paid and iii) the tax paid when the investment is sold.

The outcome is as follows:

Investment Type	Tax Paid On Deposit	Tax Paid On Growth	Tax Paid When Sold
RRSP / Pension	Before Tax	Tax Free	Fully Taxable
TFSA	After-Tax	Tax Free	Tax Free
Principle Residence	After-Tax	Tax Free	Tax Free
Life Insurance	After-Tax	Tax Free	Tax Free
RESP	After-Tax	Tax Free	Tax Free
Vacation Property	After-Tax	Taxable	Fully Taxable
Taxable Investment Account	After-Tax	Taxable	Fully–Partially Taxable
Leveraged Investment Loan	After-Tax	Taxable	Fully – Partially Taxable
Income Real Estate	After-Tax	Taxable	Fully Taxable

We can see from the above table that there are actually "three different levels to investment types": i) those investments that can be made "before tax", ii) those investments that are made after-tax but can be withdrawn tax free and iii) those investments that are made after-tax that when withdrawn are taxable (either fully as income or partially as dividends or capital gains).

The first rule of investing is simply this: Any time you can invest money prior to paying a dollar in tax, you are much more likely to end up further ahead. This means that money invested into an RRSP, Spousal RRSP or pension plan is always much more effective than investing money after-tax (level 2 or level 3 in the above table).

RRSP vs. TFSA

Now let's look at the difference between the RRSP and the TFSA. It is important to consider the following rules:

- If Nate and Natalie's "marginal tax rate" is expected to be lower in retirement then it is while they are working, the RRSP is always better than the TFSA.

- If the marginal tax rate is expected to be the same in retirement, then there is NO difference in the RRSP vs. the TFSA.

- If you are able to invest more than $5500 after-tax (i.e.: the maximum allowed for the TFSA) and the marginal tax rate in retirement is expected to be the same or less, the RRSP is the better choice due to the fact that the RRSP contribution room is likely higher than the TFSA contribution room.

- If the marginal tax rate in retirement is expected to be higher than it is today, the TFSA is the best option and offers greater flexibility when drawing income.

Can You Have Too Much in RRSPs?

Personally, I believe the answer is clearly, yes and there are several ways to answer this question:

- What is your income in relation to the Age Credit Clawback limit? By age 65, if total income from all fully taxable sources (CPP, OAS, RRSP, Pension, Rental Income) is projected to begin to exceed the Age Credit Clawback limit, then perhaps additional contributions should be made into the TFSA rather than the RRSP. Remember that this is on a per spouse basis.

- What is your income in relation to the Old Age Security Clawback Limit? By age 65, if all income sources are projected to exceed the clawback limit then perhaps additional contributions should be made into the TFSA rather than the RRSP. Remember that this is on a per spouse basis.

- What are your after-tax income needs and wants? Another benchmark to consider is to look at your projected after-tax income to be received in relation to the after-tax income you need. If your projected income exceeds the income you expect to need, then perhaps the best option is to invest into the TFSA. This may be the better choice because you can control both the timing of your withdrawals, as well as the amount withdrawn, when you draw income from the TFSA. Alternatively, when drawing income from a RRIF, the government has predetermined formulas (i.e.: the minimum RRIF rules) that determine the minimum amount that must be withdrawn each year. The government also pre-determines that you must begin to withdraw from the RRSP/RRIF by the year you turn 72. In retirement, it is always best to have as much flexibility as possible when determining the amount of income to withdraw as well as the timing of when to draw it. In this case, the TFSA has considerably more flexibility than the RRSP.

  If your projected income falls short of the income you need, and you are expected to be within the clawback zones mentioned above, then the best approach is likely to maximize your investments into the RRSP.

You see, when we add some "rules" to life's most typical decisions, and when those rules are in the context of the Killers of Wealth, we begin to see some very clear strategies that can add tens to hundreds of thousands of dollars of additional wealth over one's retirement.

Understanding Who Should Own Each Investment

When you begin to understand how our tax system works, you begin to clearly see the importance of having "two equal incomes" in retirement.

There are two goals that are important to achieve:

1. Always strive to have an equal amount of assets and an equal amount of income shared between both spouses throughout retirement.
2. Always strive to have multiple sources of income in retirement.

IN SUMMARY

Seven to Ten Years before Retirement

Nate and Natalie are 10 years prior to their retirement. They want to know if they are on track to having enough money to retire at that time. They want to know how much they should save during this time to make sure they have enough. They want to know where they should invest to get the best value for their dollar.

The typical approach is to prepare a long term retirement calculation that may be projected out to Nate and Natalie's 90th birthdays. The alternative approach, and the approach that I highly advocate, is to spend more time focusing on the shorter term details rather than the longer term generalities. You see, as the saying goes, the devil is always in the details. By focusing on the tax return, since tax is the greatest Killer of Wealth, you are able to more clearly see the tax impact of different types of income in retirement. Therefore, you are more clearly able to determine where each new dollar of savings should be allocated.

There are important rules to follow, as I've mentioned throughout this book and this chapter, that all stem from the Great Killers of Wealth. By focusing on overcoming these Killers of Wealth, you have more income and more wealth, often with less risk. By ignoring the Killers of Wealth you will always have less income combined with greater risks.

Things You Need To Know

- Your anticipated tax picture in retirement.
- How different types of investments are taxed.
- The Order of Investing Rules.
- The purpose of this process is to have more after-tax income to spend. It is not our purpose to reduce income, just the tax.

Questions You Need To Ask:

- How much after-tax income do you likely need and want in retirement?
- How does this income compare with the tax zones on the tax return?
- How does this compare with your projected savings and income projections?
- Do you need to change where you save so as to pay less tax on income in retirement?

Things You Need To Do:

- Every 12 to 18 months project forward your savings and model the income from these savings on the tax return.
- Begin this process 10 years prior to retirement.
- Follow the "Order of Investing" rules to maximize your savings and your income.
- Consider the use of other tax-advantaged investments such as a capital class structure, a T-SWP structure, prescribed annuities and "advantaged" income products.

Decisions You Need To Make:

- Depending on the number of years prior to retirement, you may need to decide between maximizing tax savings today vs. tax savings over your retirement years. In many cases you may choose to give up some tax savings today (such as not making additional RRSP deposits) in exchange for tax savings throughout retirement (by investing instead into a TFSA).

Mastery Principle

Where you invest is more important than how much you invest. We refer to this as Tactical Saving. Be forward-looking.

6

One to Two Years
Prior to Retirement

"When you can't have what you want, it's time to start wanting what you have." KATHLEEN A. SUTTON

Robert and Elizabeth are both turning 60 this year and are planning to retire but they have many questions. What will they do? Where will they live? Will they get along? Will they have enough money? Are they ready? These are the most common questions facing everyone as they approach retirement.

Robert is ready to retire. He has worked for the same company and in the same department for the past 25 years. He is tired of the day to day grind and is ready to leave it all behind. He can't wait to retire.

Elizabeth, on the other hand, is quite unsure about retirement. While she can relate to Robert's eagerness for a different life, she is concerned that a) their investments have not performed as expected and is concerned that they do not have enough money to retire, b) they will not feel comfortable seeing their income fluctuate as the value of their portfolio fluctuates, c) once they retire they may become "old" before their time and d) she and Robert will have trouble finding things to do together for the next 20 years of their life.

Robert and Elizabeth have worked hard their entire life and they want to enjoy the fruits of their labour. At this time the grass seems to be greener on the other side of the retirement fence, but is it really? Are they more excited about leaving the work force than they are about their future lifestyle?

THE ISSUES

Are Robert and Elizabeth ready to retire "financially"? Are Robert and Elizabeth ready to retire "psychologically"? These are two completely different issues.

Are they looking forward to the same things or do they each have a different vision of retirement? Do they each know what is important to the other?

The extent to which both spouses are in sync with the other in terms of the ideal retirement vision is extremely important. This does not mean that both spouses need to spend every waking moment together doing the same thing. Actually, for many it is quite the opposite. A shared vision for retirement is a very important issue. This was first mentioned in Chapter 1 and summarized as Mastery Principle 4: The Masters Work As A Team.

What will be the plan for today and how does this compare with the longer term plan? What should the plan include? How far in the future should they plan?

When building a plan for retirement it must include many components. These components are similar to what you need today to enjoy your life to the fullest. It would often include your health, your activities and your relationships. When developing your plan for retirement, it is very important to consider each of these components, both over the short term and the long term.

How important is it to have as many "guarantees" as possible throughout their retirement years?

Having a vision and a plan is one thing. Having a realistic, low risk plan is something else. Keeping your risks low in retirement is a very important issue.

Are you really ready? Are you set in your plans?...Or is something holding you back?

To resolve the questions that are in your mind today, you must first develop a vision for what your ideal retirement, for the next three to five years in particular, will look like. This vision should be reviewed and discussed ideally every one to three years. In Chapter 1 we talked about creating an ideal plan to live a well balanced life. This chapter demonstrates steps to develop your vision for this plan. This chapter also reinforces the importance of Mastery Principle 2: Being externally focused.

THE SOLUTIONS

The solution is really quite simple: it is important to have a picture in your mind of what your ideal retirement is all about. For example, on the great cruise ship of life, if the ship doesn't have a clear idea of where it's going and how it's going to get there, then the result is random.

In short you leave your future – a time when you could be at your most vulnerable personal state – up to chance. You will definitely end up somewhere, but you won't know where you will be until you arrive, and you may not like the company you'll be forced to keep in your new environment, either.

Retirement is a new phase of life, perhaps a phase that is unlike any you have experienced before. This is scary for some and exciting for others. This is a time and place to which some cannot wait to arrive, while it is something that others insist on postponing as long as possible. Some will enjoy retirement, some will excel at retirement and others will fail miserably.

As you know with all things in life, it is ultimately up to you to decide your own level of success. Your level of success will depend on how well you prepare for this new phase of life and how well you adapt along the way.

Let's get started by building a compelling vision of your "ideal" retired life going forward:

1. What is a Retirement Vision?
2. How do you create a vision for retirement?
3. What should this vision include?
4. Why can transitioning to retirement be so challenging?
5. How do you know if you are ready to retire?

What is a Retirement Vision?

Very simply, a retirement vision is a picture of your "ideal" life moving forward. This picture is extremely important for several reasons:

- Many people are unsure if they will be "happy" in retirement. The only way to know if you will be happy is to have a picture of what your "ideal" retirement period will look like.

- "Retirement" is a long period of time with five different phases. To be happy in retirement it is extremely important to anticipate and plan for these changes. People are unhappy in retirement when they are ill prepared for these phases and an unexpected crisis, illness or death occurs.

- A vision for retirement helps to identify the expenses you will have. By identifying the expenses, you will be able to determine the income you will require.

- A vision is important because it will help you to retire "to" something important and meaningful to you. Alternatively, some people can't wait to retire from their current job. In these instances they are retiring "from" something. If you are retiring "from" something rather than "to" something, you may find your level of happiness is much less than what you thought it would be. A vision is extremely important to provide interest, excitement and meaning to you.

How do You Create a Vision for Retirement?

To create a unique and compelling vision for retirement, you will need to follow three important steps:

1. Make a list of the Top 100 things that are most important to you.
2. Plot this list onto a "Lifeline" chart that shows the incremental time between today and the day you die.
3. Set some goals. Make sure you cover all of the important aspects of your vision: your health, your relationships and your activities.

Now let's take a look at each of these steps in more detail:

The Top 100

Make a list of all the things you'd love to do before you die. A recent movie has referred to this as the "Bucket List", the things you'd love to do before you "kick the bucket". Try to list as many things as you can such as:

*   The places you'd love to see.
*   The things you'd love to do.
*   The people you'd like to visit.
*   The number of times you'd like to have the grandkids over for a sleepover.
*   The number of days each year you'd like to spend at the lake.
*   New things you'd like to learn.
*   Relationships you'd like to mend.
*   Problems you'd like to solve.
*   Things you'd like to do on your own.
*   Things you'd like to do with your spouse.
*   Contributions you'd like to make (to the community).
*   Time you'd like to volunteer.

If the list is full you will never be short of ideas. Do this on your own and then with your spouse. Compare your lists and set some priorities.

The Lifeline

This next step is important because it takes the list of things you identified in your Top 100 list and begins to set some time frames. For example:

*   Draw a line from left to right on a large piece of paper. The far left end of the line is where you are in your life today.

- Write down your name and your age on the far left end of the line.

- Now take a look at the far right end of the line. The far right end of the line will be the day you die. For the sake of discussion enter age 85 on the far right end of the line.

- This leaves us the space in between the far left and the far right, the space between today and the day you die. The space in between is the time available to do all of the 100 things you'd like to do before you die.

- Now fill in the gaps between where you are today (on the far left) and the age you noted on the right end of the line. Mark a spot on the line for every 3 year period. If you are 60 today create a point on the life line for ages 63, 66, 69, 72, 75, 78, 81 and 84.

- Enter your age above each 3 year increment.

- Now begin to fill in the spaces under each 3 year increment. Enter those places you'd like to see, activities you'd like to do, people you'd like to spend time with and things you'd like to learn. Try to enter everything on your Top 100 List. If you can't enter everything, then determine which items on the Top 100 List are most important.

- When you see your "lifeline" you will begin to develop the "ideal" vision for your life from this point forward. If this vision is exciting to you, then you know you are on the right track. If it is not exciting to you, then make the necessary changes.

By following these steps you have painted a picture of what you will do with your time at each stage of your life moving forward. Seeing the time slip away across the lifeline can be very sobering and create a very compelling sense of urgency.

Now take what you have done and raise it to the next level:

- Enter the name and age of your spouse over these same periods of time.

- Do this again for your children and your grandchildren.

What do you see? Will you change the timing and urgency of some of your own activities due to the ages of others? In most situations the answer will be "Yes". When you begin to take into account the age of others, your lifeline vision will most definitely change. When your oldest grandchild is 10, should you plan a trip to Disney World?

Now look at the overall lifeline one more time. How does it look? Are you excited? Is this the picture of your ideal life moving forward? Do you and your spouse share the same vision? If not, where are the compromises?

Here's an example of what your lifeline could look like:

	Current	Years 1-3	Years 4-6	Years 7-9	Years 10+
Bob	60	63	66	69	70+
Mary	58	61	64	67	68+
Son	30	33	36	39	40+
Daughter	27	30	33	36	37+
Grandson	4	7	10	13	14+
Granddaughter	2	5	8	11	12+

	Current	Years 1-3	Years 4-6	Years 7-9	Years 10+
Bob	60	63	66	69	70+
Mary	58	61	64	67	68+
Son	30	33	36	39	40+
Daughter	27	30	33	36	37+
Grandson	4	7	10	13	14+
Granddaughter	2	5	8	11	12+

Milestones:	Retirement		65th B-day		Son's 40th B-day

Top 100:					
Health	Lose 10 lbs	Reach target weight			
Travel		Italy	Australia	Europe	Disney
Work			Part Time	Fully Retire	
Volunteer	2 days a week at a children's hospital.				
Sports		Curl, Golf	Curl, Golf	Curl, Golf	
Fitness		Walk 5 times a week	Bike 50 kms		

Set Some Goals

It is now time to make sure you have set some goals in all of the most important areas of your life.

- **Your health:** You see from this vision just how important it will be to have your health over time. If you are planning on being active throughout your 70s and into your 80s, a healthy diet with regular exercise is critical to your ability to live out your ideal vision. As you reflect on your "lifeline", make some notes underneath and perhaps at every interval, state your health and exercise related goals.

- **Your relationships:** You may dedicate space on your lifeline for i) activities with other friends and family, ii) time spent enhancing your relationship with your spouse, and iii) repairing broken relationships with long lost friends or family. When your relationships are all intact, you are often having the most fun and you are the most at peace with things. When relationships are broken and conflict persists, it is easy to become muddled, de-energized, isolated and miserable. Therefore, when building an ideal vision it is important and valuable to commit time on your lifeline to enhancing your relationships.

- **Your activities:** Make a list of the regular activities you'd like to participate in each year. This may include sporting activities that you participate in at various times throughout each year, hobbies or volunteer activities in the community. You may wish to continue to work part time for several years or run a small business or do some extra consulting work. All of these are examples of the activities you will be doing to keep busy, interested and engaged in the world around you.

- **Your milestones:** Milestones will be specific dates or points in time when specific events will take place. For example, high school or university graduation (kids and grandkids), marriage dates or dates in which your income may change for one reason or another.

Summary: How to Create a Vision For Retirement

At the end of this process you have created a line marked by three year increments. Above this line will be the names and ages of the people closest to you. Below this line may be several rows. The first row may be your "Top 100". The next row may be your "health" list. The next row may be your "relationships" list. The next row may be your "activities" list. The next row may be your list of milestones.

By following these steps you have created a very compelling "vision" of your life going forward. Sit back and take some time to live with this vision. How does it make you feel? What would you change? If you could add anything, what would you add? If you could take anything away, what would you take away?

What Should Your Vision Include?

When mapping out your vision, consider the following issues:

- **Should you retire all at once or should you retire gradually?** For many people, work helps to bring meaning, purpose and a sense of fulfillment to life. Work in and of itself may not be the issue for you, rather, it may be the type of work you do or the amount of work you do. If you were in control of your time and your work, would you be more satisfied with your life? Would you make more money? If so, then perhaps you will want to think about retiring gradually over time. Perhaps you do not need to stop working at all. Perhaps all you need is to gain control over your work.

With this in mind, it is important to be aware of a new provision available for people who are members of a defined benefit pension plan in Canada. You have the option today of receiving some "pension income" while still working part time for the same company and continuing to contribute to the same pension plan. If you had this type of guaranteed basic income coming in month after month, how would that change the way you view your work, your time and your life?

- **Should you and your spouse retire at the same time?** As mentioned previously, you are planning for the retirement of not just one individual but for two. You may choose to retire today while your spouse may choose to retire in a few years' time. This may be an excellent consideration since the additional employment income will give you and your spouse the opportunity to do the things you most want to do in the early years of retirement.

- **Should you sell your business?** Many small to mid-sized businesses produce a significant amount of "cash flow". This cash flow can give the owner(s) an above average income month after month. Yet, if the business were sold, the net proceeds after tax may not be enough to replace this income. It is important for business owners to weigh the financial implications of keeping the business alive or selling it outright today. In many cases the business as a long term going concern is worth more to the retiree then it is if it were wound down or sold.

Each of these three points should be considered when developing the ideal vision and plan for retirement.

Why can Transitioning to Retirement be so Challenging?

To truly *Master Your Retirement*, it is extremely important to understand why "transitioning to retirement" can be such a challenge. If you understand the challenges then you can prepare to address these challenges in advance.

- **Retirement is a long period of time.** Due to the fact that retirement may be 15 to 25 years in length, many people find it difficult to fathom what they would do over such a long period of time. By working through each of the three steps in the "Retirement Vision" process noted previously in this chapter, and by understanding the Phases of Retirement, you begin to realize that this period of time can go by very quickly. The "Retirement Vision" process is your best approach to creating a compelling vision of your life and a strong sense of urgency.

- **Retirement, for some, may be viewed as the beginning of the end.** For many people retirement is viewed as being just one step closer to the grave yard. Due to this fear of death, some people give up on life completely. They assume that tomorrow will be their last, so there is no point in starting anything new today. To overcome this fear, you must go back to your Retirement Vision and you must assume that you will live longer than you expect. Yes, you must plan for longevity. By planning for longevity you will be creating a long list of all of the things that are important to you. By creating this list you will also create a keen sense of urgency to get through this list.

- **Retirement means sickness.** It is difficult, if not impossible, to ignore the fact that life is drawing to an end. With every new ache or pain it is impossible not to think in terms of cancer, heart disease or stroke. Yet, ironically, the more one ponders life's great ailments, the more likely these can be self-fulfilling outcomes. Before you know it, time has passed and opportunities have been missed. If death and disease is something that pre-occupies your thoughts, perhaps you really should approach life with a greater sense of urgency. It is also best to do a financial audit for when illness strikes. By doing this work you will begin to alleviate your fears in this area and help you move forward. Don't let health issues distract you. Confront them.

- **Your employment income ends.** For the first time in your life your income will come from sources other than "work". Your entire income will now come from your investments, pensions and government benefits. It can be extremely difficult for some to adjust to this new reality. It can be extremely difficult to "trust" that your income will always be there. This is often a huge source of stress for many couples in retirement. To rely on investment returns from this point forward can often create more fear than certainty because of the complexity of the investment world and the often scary fluctuations of the stock market. If you are nervous about your income, there are many ways available to create more certainty.

- **Retirement changes your sense of who you are.** Retirement can be difficult because you stop working. Ironic, isn't it? You strive to get to a time and place when you no longer have to work, yet stopping work may result in more stress. Work gives a sense of accomplishment, a sense of contribution, a sense of usefulness and, for many, a sense of who you are. For most of our lives, our sense of identity is defined by education, career, job title or the nature of our business. While raising a family your identity may also be linked to the activities of your children or by the community in which you live. Yet, when you retire, both your work identity and your parental identity may diminish or cease to exist. Who are you as you enter this next phase of life? Who are you without your kids? Who are you without your job? Who are you without your business? When you retire your sense of identity will shift. Getting your mind around this "shift in identity" may take some time.

- **Personal satisfaction may not come from retirement but from control related issues.** Many people believe that "work" is the thing that we need to get away from, and this is a problem. "Work" in itself is not really the problem. The real challenge is to have control of your time and your destiny and to have the "choice" to do what you want when you want to do it. Some form of "work" or "meaningful activity" is vital to happiness and overall retirement success. For those who do not recognize this reality, retirement may be extremely difficult. It is therefore important to consider all of your options. Maybe the best approach is to gradually retire over time.

- **Are you healthy enough to retire?** At this time of your life your energy, your health and your physical strength is not what it has been in the past. To fully "Master" this time of life, attention to your physical health is of utmost importance. Without a reasonable amount of good health, you may find that you will begin to miss out on gatherings and activities with family and friends. This can result in the feeling of isolation and resentment that can in turn create greater negative health effects. Spending time reflecting on your health, your activities and your relationships is just as important as reflecting on your investments and different sources of income.

How do You Know if You are Ready to Retire?

The best answer to this question comes from your "Retirement Vision". Is the vision compelling, meaningful, exciting and energizing? If so, then you know that you are truly retiring "to" something rather than just retiring "from" something.

When you think of retirement, do you think of "just getting by" or can you get excited about "mastering your retirement"? Can you look forward to doing something new? Or are you just focused on getting away from what ails you today?

If you answered positively to these questions, you are psychologically ready for retirement. Remember, even though you may feel that you are ready to retire, this "readiness" should not be driven by how tired or frustrated you are today with the daily grind. Odds are that retirement will bring its own challenges and frustrations. To see your way through these inevitable challenges, it is critical to have your goals, your dreams, your vision and your passions clearly identified.

Are you financially ready to retire? To answer this question, allow me to pose other questions:

- Were you financially ready to buy your first home?
- Were you financially ready to be married?
- Were you financially ready to start a family?
- Were you financially ready to have your children attend university?

I think you get my point. I believe that most people will never have "enough" money to retire, regardless of how much wealth they really have. Therefore, the purpose of the *Master Your Retirement* approach is two-fold: it focuses on both your income and the preservation and transition of your capital.

In short, you want to make sure your overall after-tax income is as large as possible while keeping your sources of that income as safe from dangerous eroders as possible.

> *We focus on after-tax income because it does not matter what you have, it only matters what you keep.*

IN SUMMARY

One to Two Years Prior to Retirement

Things You Need To Know

- You will know that you are truly ready to retire when you have a clear "vision" of what your retirement will look like.
- To *Master Your Retirement* you need to find a balance between your health, your relationships and your activities.
- The financial objective is to do all that you can to maximize after-tax income by minimizing income taxes. This issue alone can have the greatest impact on Mastering Your Retirement.
- You will never have enough money to retire. You will always feel that you need more.
- There are seven main reasons why people find it difficult to retire. To *Master Your Retirement* you need to be aware of these reasons and confront them accordingly.

Questions You Need To Ask

- Are you retiring so as to "get away from" a bad situation at work OR are you retiring "to" a clear vision and journey that you are excited to embark upon?

- If you had more "control" over your working environment, would this influence how and when you retire?
- Do you "need" to continue to work so as to feel that you are remaining active and involved in the community or for your own enjoyment? (This is a very important fact for many people.)
- Do you and your spouse have a different "vision" of retirement? What do you need to do to find the ideal "compromise"?
- Which of the seven challenges of transitioning to retirement apply to you? Your spouse? What do you need to do to overcome these issues?

Things You Need To Do

- Follow the three step Retirement Vision process.
  - Step 1: Begin making a list of your Top 100.
  - Step 2: Begin to map out your Lifeline.
  - Step 3: Set goals in terms of health, activities, relationships and milestones.
- Have your spouse do the same thing and compare your answers.

Decisions You Need To Make

- Decide and commit to take all of the necessary steps, as outlined in the introduction to *Master Your Retirement*.
- Decide and commit to take the time to complete the Retirement Vision process.
- Don't be firm on any specific retirement date or plan until you have gone through the entire book and spent time working through the various processes.
- Decide to keep an open mind.

Mastery Principle

As the saying goes "failing to plan ahead" is akin to "planning to fail". Transitioning into retirement is one of the most significant events of your life. Take the time necessary to build a clear "vision" and you will be rewarded with greater health, closer relationships and a more fulfilling life. Thus, it is important for spouses to work together as a team and be externally focused.

7

The First Two Years
of Retirement

*"When we are motivated by goals that have deep meaning,
by dreams that need completion, by pure love that needs expressing – then
we truly live life."* GREG ANDERSON

Mark and Joanne are now retired. They have done a great job preparing for retirement, but now reality begins to set in. They are very excited about the things they will be doing, the places they will be going and the people they will be spending time with along the way, but it still seems a little surreal.

Mark and Joanne still have some concerns, many of which may never go away. Who knows if things will really turn out as planned? Are their goals realistic? Are they taking too much risk?

They have seen some of their friends jump into retirement only to find that they have to cut back on their plans at a later time, which is always difficult to do.

Mark and Joanne have entered the first two years of retirement.

THE ISSUES

Congratulations! You've made it! You have now entered retirement. So how does it feel? Does it feel like you expected? Are things coming together as planned? Are there any surprises? Is anything keeping you up at night?

The first two years of retirement is still a time of great transition. You are creating new routines, trying out new activities, continuing with some and eliminating others. So now what? You've done all of this planning, where do you go from here?

THE SOLUTIONS

In the first two years of retirement, there are seven things I recommend you pay close attention to:

1. Your Tax Picture.
2. Your Government Benefits.
3. Your Property.
4. Your Portfolio.
5. Your Health.
6. Your Activities.
7. Your Relationships.

In other words, this is not necessarily a time just to sit back and relax. Well, actually it is, but what I mean is that you can't put things on auto-pilot. Now is a time for reflection and assessment, and each of these areas are key to an abundant and exciting future.

Your taxes need to be optimized, your government benefits need to be maximized, how you will use your various properties needs to be explored, and while your portfolio is very vulnerable at this stage it will be your activities, your health and your relationships that will make the next phase of retirement so fulfilling.

Remember, we're focused on Mastery and not mediocrity here because you may have only one chance to really get things right.

This chapter will provide you with a check list of things to consider and review during the first two years of retirement. But you will notice that we don't recommend that you make any significant changes during these first two years. We believe it is important to live out your retirement vision and let it take shape around you. The right answers will come to you in time. This is consistent with Mastery Principle 1, found in Chapter 1: Making Gradual Changes over Longer Periods of Time.

Your Tax Picture

In Phase 1, of the 5 Phases of Retirement, you spent time beginning to layer your income and model future scenarios on the tax return. Since you started to do this, however, tax rates have been indexed, tax credits have been modified and changes may have been made to your various sources of income. So now is the time to update things once again. As a matter of fact, it is important to do this every six to 12 months at a minimum.

You begin by asking the following questions:

- Do my spouse and I have two equal incomes now that we are retired? Remember, two smaller and equal incomes will always pay less tax than one larger income.

- If not, are there ways to reduce taxes by "splitting income" between us?

- What income sources are you drawing from today? Are you drawing income from a pension plan, Canada Pension Plan retirement income benefits, RRSP withdrawals or are you receiving income from a RRIF, LRIF, PRIF or LIF? Depending on your current age, some or all of these income sources could be split equally with your spouse, thereby potentially reducing the tax paid on this income.

- How old are you today? Depending on the sources of income identified above, you will be able to split up to 50% of this income with your spouse. Income from a pension plan can be split with a spouse at any age; however, income from a RRIF, LRIF, LIF, PRIF or annuity cannot be split with the spouse until the owner of the investment reaches age 65. This calculation takes place at the end of the year on your tax return. Your Canada Pension Plan benefits can be split equally once both of you begin to draw these benefits.

- Do you qualify for any tax credits? If you are age 65 or older you will qualify for the "age credit". You want to make sure that each spouse maximizes this credit each and every year.

- Are any credits or benefits being clawed back? Once your income begins to exceed the Age Credit limit you will begin to lose this credit on your lower levels of income. This means that your taxes will go up on your lower levels of income. What about Old Age Security? If you are over age 65 and you are receiving Old Age Security income benefits, your total taxable income needs to remain below the OAS clawback level or else you will begin to pay this benefit back to the federal government. If you are losing any of your credits, you want to look for ways of rearranging your income so that you can maximize these benefits. These figures are provided in the Technical Appendix.

- What is your marginal tax rate? How close are you to the next tax bracket level above and below your current income? Are you just above the next lower level? If so, then is there anything you can do to modify the type of income received or take further advantage of the income splitting opportunities available so as to get your total income completely down to the next lower category?

Up to now you have projected what your income may look like in retirement. However, this is an on-going process that is always changing. Ideally, you will spend time twice a year i) reviewing your income from the previous year in April (when your tax return is filed) and then ii) reviewing your current years income in both April and November so that you have time to make any necessary changes so as to minimize tax for the current year.

Since tax is life's single greatest expense, paying continuous attention to the tax you pay is immensely important to make sure you have the most amount of money available to live the life you so desire.

Your Government Benefits

In this section we will look at several government benefit programs that will be of importance to you: Canada Pension Plan, Old Age Security, the Age Credit and the Disability Tax Credit.

The Canada Pension Plan (CPP)

There are three key concepts to consider with regard to your CPP retirement benefit.

1. Maximize your benefits. When calculating your CPP benefit, the federal government will take into account your number of working years. They will eliminate the seven lowest income earning years when calculating your benefit. This is good. Even better, the new CPP rules launched in January 2011 will allow one to increase the number of "low income/drop out years" to a maximum of eight by 2014. There is another benefit called the Child Rearing Provision. If you were out of the work force due to the fact that you stayed home to raise your children, you can also request to have those years removed from your pension income calculation. Review your CPP statement to ensure it is accurate and to ensure that the years in which you did not contribute are eliminated from the calculation. To do this, contact the Service Canada office nearest you and ask for an updated CPP printout, review it and then discuss it with one of the representatives to ensure you are receiving the maximum benefit available to you.

2. Begin benefits at age 60, 65 or 70? The amount of retirement benefit you receive is based on your contributions and the number of years you contributed. The maximum monthly benefit available today is included in the Technical Appendix. This is the maximum benefit available to you if you work to age 65. If you begin to draw your monthly benefits prior to age 65 they will be reduced. The pension reduction rules at this time are being modified. The 2011 rules state that those retiring in 2011 or earlier will see their maximum pension benefit reduced by 6% per year for every year prior to age 65. If you are 60 years old, this would mean that your pension benefit

would be reduced by 30%. However, beginning with those who retire in 2012, the amount by which the monthly pension amount is reduced will be increased gradually each year until 2016 when the new rules will be a 7.2% reduction per year. .

Beginning in January 2011 changes are also being made to the monthly benefit you receive if you wait to draw your CPP pension benefit until age 65 or later (maximum deferral to age 70). In 2011 the monthly increase is .57% and by 2013 this will have grown to .7%. If you waited to age 70 to draw your pension benefit, the maximum benefit would be increased by 0.7% per month or 8.4% per year. The maximum payment received would be approximately 50% higher per month when you reach age 70 compared to if you took the lower amount at age 65.

Some may wish to draw benefits from the CPP as soon as possible if, by doing so: i) it allows you to defer drawing any income from your other investments (thus allowing them to grow further over time) and ii) due to the potentially smaller survivor benefit and death benefit, receiving as much CPP benefit as early as possible will help to ensure you get good value for the money you've invested.

As with all things, every situation is unique and will need to be assessed based on your specific situation.

3. Split your CPP retirement benefit with your spouse. Depending on your specific situation, it may be beneficial to split some of your CPP retirement benefit with your spouse. To do so you need to apply to have this done at the Services Canada office. In general, you have the ability to combine your two pension amounts together and then divide the two equally so each spouse receives approximately the same amount. Note that in some cases, due to the approach used by CPP, you may not end up with exactly equal amounts.

The New Rules: Several additional changes to the CPP retirement benefit are currently taking place.

•   As mentioned above, beginning in 2012 the amount by which your benefit will be reduced or increased will be changed depending on when you begin to draw your pension. This makes delaying the drawing of your pension more advantageous, particularly if you do live for a long period of time. In most situations today, the best approach is to delay drawing your CPP until at least age 65.

•   Beginning in 2012, you can elect to draw your CPP amount so long as you are age 60 or older. Once you apply, regardless of whether you are currently working or not, you can begin to receive your monthly benefit. However, should you continue to work between age 60 and 65 you will need to continue to contribute to the CPP. When you do, these additional contributions will not impact your current monthly benefit. Instead, a "post retirement benefit" will be set up for you and you will begin to receive benefits from this side account over time. Once you reach age 65 you can choose whether you wish to continue to make contributions into this "post retirement benefit" or not. If you are still working at age 65, you could choose to no longer contribute to the "post retirement benefit". If you choose to continue to contribute, then your employer will be obligated to contribute as well. By age 70, no further contributions can be made. The amount of the post retirement benefit will be equal to 1/40th of the maximum pension amount depending on the amount actually contributed and the age of the individual. Our analysis indicates that the post retirement benefit amount received is far less than the discount rate applied when taking CPP early. Therefore, we believe that most, if not all, people are better off by delaying the start of their CPP retirement benefit to age 65 or older. The exception to this rule will be situations where there is a clear and definite shortened life expectancy.

Old Age Security (OAS)

This is a government funded program available to all Canadians age 65 and over who have lived in Canada a minimum of 10 years. It is important to note that OAS is different from the CPP. During your employment years you and your employer each contributed to the CPP. The amount of CPP benefit you receive today is based on those contributions. However, OAS is funded from the general tax revenues of the Federal Government and is generally the same for everyone who qualifies. Old Age Security is exactly that. It is meant to provide additional financial security in retirement. Therefore, if you earn too much taxable income in retirement you will have to pay some of the Old Age Security benefit received back to the government. This is what we refer to as the OAS clawback. Any taxable income earned above the clawback amount will trigger, on your tax return, a repayment of 15% of every dollar earned above this threshold. For example, $10,000 of additional taxable income above the clawback amount will require $1,500 of OAS to be paid back to the Federal Government.

Over 20 years of retirement, the amount of OAS received can add up to a significant amount of money. Over 20 years of retirement, when you include a 2% level of inflation per year, this could add up to over $300,000 of additional retirement income for the couple. Needless to say, this is not something that you want to take lightly.

The clawback threshold is indexed with inflation and will usually increase by 1% to 2% each year, which is beneficial. However, since the inflation number will change each year, the prudent citizen who is Mastering Retirement will want to keep track of this figure and plan their income wisely throughout each year.[3]

Tax Credits

A tax credit is a calculation that directly reduces the amount of tax paid, as opposed to a tax deduction which reduces taxable income (e.g.: an RRSP contribution). A tax credit of $5,000 is multiplied by 15% to equal $750. If your tax owing before the credit is claimed is $2,000, after the credit is claimed your tax owing will be only $1,250. Tax credits are highly advantageous.

The most common tax credits are as follows. The current figures are provided in the Technical Appendix:

- **Personal amount**: All tax filers receive a basic personal amount from Federal tax on a basic amount of annual income. This amount is indexed with inflation. If one spouse does not have any income and you are unable to split some of your income with this individual, a spousal credit for this amount will be added to your personal amount.

- **Age amount**: Available to those over age 65 with less than the Age Credit Clawback amount in income (note: this amount is indexed and changes annually). Over 20 years the tax savings could add up to close to $40,000. To minimize the clawback you must pay attention to the amount and type of income you receive above the clawback level.

- **Pension income amount**: The first $2,000 of pension income is tax-free for each spouse. This is the equivalent of $600 in tax credits each and every year in retirement. Over 20 years this will result in approximately $12,000 in tax savings for the couple. This amount is not clawed back.

- **Caregiver amount**: Do you take care of an adult who is infirm and dependent on you? Does this person reside with you? If so, you may be eligible to claim a "caregiver" tax credit.

- **Infirm dependent amount:** In the event you are taking care of another adult individual who is unable to care for themselves due to a permanent mental or physical disability, you may claim some of these expenses as part of the Infirm Dependent tax credit.

- **Family Caregiver Tax Credit**: In the 2011 Federal Budget a $2,000 Family Caregiver Tax Credit is to be incorporated into the amounts noted above.

---

[3] See Appendix regarding postponing OAS if full clawback to age 70

- **Disability Tax Credit:** The maximum credit available to a disabled person is $7,766 (in 2014). The application for this credit requires certification from a medical practitioner.

- **Medical expenses:** The credit is based on the taxpayer's allowable medical expenses for any 12-month period ending in the taxation year minus 3% of the taxpayer's net income on line 236 (up to an annually indexed maximum amount). Because the claim is reduced by 3% of the taxpayer's net income, it is often best to claim the amount on the return of the lower-income taxpayer, unless that taxpayer is not taxable.

- **Charitable donations:** The first $200 of total charitable gifts is eligible for a 15% Federal credit and the remainder of the gifts is eligible for a 29% Federal tax credit. When combined with the Provincial credits these amounts add up to your marginal tax rate. You may carry forward donations for five years and by doing so may receive better tax treatment for your donations.

As you can see, these credits, over long periods of time, can add up to be many tens of thousands of dollars, if not more.

Your Property

Your home is your castle, it may also be one of your most valuable financial assets and it has some very unique tax advantages. In addition to your home you may own a time share, a cottage and even rental property. You may need to sell, or you may wish to sell, one or more properties so as to use this money to generate income.

The best advice I can offer as it relates to real estate property, is to do nothing with it in the first two years of retirement.

As mentioned previously, the first two years is a time of transition. It is a time when you begin to discover what you "really" want to do and who you most want to do it with. Selling a property is a very significant financial event given the taxes that may be involved, real estate commissions and lawyer fees. Selling and buying property can create many tens of thousands of dollars of lost "equity" just through these types of fees. Needless to say, you really want to be sure that what you are doing is what you really want to do. That is why we suggest to our clients to not make any quick decisions about where they will live and property they wish to buy or to sell.

Alternatively, we encourage our clients to "test drive" a lifestyle, a property or a location. Go to that location several times over the years to really make sure that this is a place that you will want to go back to.

During the first two years of retirement, try to stick with the status quo. Try to avoid making quick, impulsive decisions. When the time is right, you will know that it is the right time to act and you will know where you ultimately wish to live throughout the year.

Your Portfolio

Let me be perfectly clear, the most vulnerable time for your portfolio is the first two years of retirement. The reasons for this are simple:

- You may never have as much money invested as you do the day you retire. This may be your "peak" wealth.
- Your retirement period ahead of you is never longer than on the day you retire.
- A decline in the value of your investments in the first two years may be something from which you never recover.
- A decline in the value of your investments, combined with income withdrawals, may also be an event from which you may never recover.

Therefore, the investment strategy you use during the two years leading up to retirement as well as the first two years of retirement should likely be quite defensive.

It is important that you play a very active role in understanding exactly how your money is invested.

You will want to ask questions such as:

- If the market were to drop by 15%, can you tell me how much my portfolio may drop in value? My advice is for you to encourage your advisor to demonstrate this outcome, not just answer it with a general response. In so many words: prove it!
- If interest rates rise or fall, how will this impact my portfolio?
- If the value of the Canadian currency rises or falls, what impact will that have on my portfolio?
- If the economy slows down during this period of time, how will my portfolio adapt to these changing circumstances?

By asking these questions you are creating a "stress test" on your portfolio. This test helps to quantify how your portfolio will perform during various scenarios. This will help you determine if the portfolio's current design is right for you.

Now, when going through this process, one of the outcomes is that you may just not know what will happen to the portfolio in the event of a 15% market decline. This is not a good answer. You may not know what will happen because much of the success will depend on the third party money manager (i.e.: the managers of your mutual funds). In my view, this is also not good. It is important to recognize that a mutual fund money manager does not know you or your personal situation. They are managing money only with a mid to longer term time frame and with the "market" in mind. Their decisions are not based on your personal circumstances. Personally, I have a problem with this.

While this type of third party money management approach may be beneficial 70% to 80% of the time, it is the 20% to 30% period of which I believe you need to be more wary. As we have all experienced in the past, large portfolio losses can occur quickly over short periods of time. These are the times that you want to protect yourself against.

As a result, I recommend you consider several steps when reviewing your portfolio over time, but in particularly during the first two years of retirement:

- Have no more than 30% of your portfolio in third party mutual funds, particularly mutual funds that invest in the stock market in Canada and around the world.

- Meet with your portfolio advisor so that you understand exactly everything held in your account.

- Use a "creeping stop loss" strategy on your individual stocks or exchange traded fund investments. A "stop loss" is an automatic sell order that is triggered when the value of the investment drops to a particular level. Over time as the security rises in value you can continue to increase the "stop loss" so that it protects the growth you have earned.

- Invest in a balanced investment mix: focus on investments that generate income (dividends, interest).

There is a lot of opportunity and uncertainty in today's investment environment. The best advice I can offer is to be actively involved with your money. Understand what you are investing in. Understand where the risks are. Work closely with your advisors and be confident in asking a lot of questions.

If you don't feel comfortable with something,
then ask a question or make a change.

Your Health, Activities and Relationships

Finally we get to the most important stuff. I know what you're thinking, what could be more fun than tax, government benefits, real estate and portfolios? I know, I'm with you on that one. But believe it or not, when you pay attention to the details of your tax, government benefits, real estate and portfolio, you will have more money, less risk and greater peace of mind. For most people, this gives them the freedom and comfort to spend their income with confidence, doing the things they most wish to do.

It will be no surprise to you to know that when the money stuff is uncertain or at risk, most people tend to withdraw. By this I mean that they may withdraw from activities, family and friends. They may choose to isolate themselves, which can cause further relationship and health issues.

Personally I find it amusing when I see a retirement article or book that emphatically states "it's not about the money".

But hey, let's be clear. It is about the money: slow, steady growth in both income and capital, that protects you from wild fluctuations in the "market" so that you can have a safe and predictable income in retirement to do the things you most want to do. Now we have come full circle. When you deal with the Great Killers of Wealth, you ultimately come to the same conclusion: by minimizing taxes, fees and the impact of inflation, you will have a reliable, low risk income in retirement.

This in turn gives you the confidence to do the things you most want to do, and helps you avoid unnecessary worry and related health issues.

Your health, your activities and your relationships should always be very purposeful. What you do, how you do it, when you do it and who you do it with, are all components that will bring you great joy, happiness and peace in your retirement years.

So, during the first two years in particular, keep track of these things. Keep track of your physical fitness activities, eating and sleeping habits, activities that are fun, activities that are stimulating and make note of the people you most like doing those things with. This will help to bring great clarity and purpose to your years.

Remember, this is all about Mastery: getting the most out of all that life has to offer.

IN SUMMARY

The First Two Years of Retirement

In this chapter we discussed several aspects of Phase 2 of the Phases of Retirement. Phase 2 is the all important first two years of retirement. Phase 2 recognizes that this is still a period of transition, as you begin to feel comfortable with this new stage in life.

Things You Need To Know

- The tax return ultimately influences the design of your investment portfolio.
- The tax return influences how and when you draw income.
- Managing your tax return is about understanding the marginal tax rate levels for your province, the clawback zones and how different investment income is taxed.
- Old Age Security is one of the single largest government benefits you could receive in retirement. Your total benefits could be close to $300,000 of additional income throughout your retirement years (based on two people over 20 years).
- There are three key tax zones for those age 65 and over: Zone 1 – Income up to the Age Credit clawback, Zone 3 – Where Old Age Security begins to be clawed back. This leaves Zone 2 in the middle. Ideally, any income above the Age Credit clawback per spouse should be a more tax-efficient source of income.
- Be familiar with the tax credits available to help you reduce tax.

Questions You Need To Ask

- How much after-tax income do I (we) need to live on each month?
- What are the marginal rate tax zones in Canada? In my province?
- Which of the three tax zones am I in today?
- What is my ideal tax zone (to reduce taxes and/or clawbacks)?
- Are we taking advantage of all of the available tax credits?
- Do I need to restructure my current portfolio design and income strategy so as to reduce my tax payable?

Things You Need To Do

- Review your last two years of tax returns to assess if you have missed claiming certain credits. If you have, refile your returns.

- With your advisors, discuss and review alternative ways by which you can draw income from your investment portfolio to reduce taxes on the tax return.

- Plan ahead by looking at where you are investing money today. If you continue to add to your RRSP investments are you inviting the OAS clawback to appear?

Decisions You Need To Make

- Commit to reviewing and beating the Killers of Wealth on a continuous basis.

- Do we really need to make any "real estate" decisions at this time?

- Are we spending our time in the best possible way? If not, what would we change?

- Are we comfortable with the security of our money? If not, what would we change and why? How would this change improve our chances against the Killers of Wealth?

Mastery Principle

Take your time to make your decisions wisely. Making quick changes during a period of uncertainty can be a quick way for you to lose much of your hard earned wealth. Therefore, there are many benefits to making gradual changes to your plans over a longer period of time.

8

The Healthy Years

"When patterns are broken, new worlds emerge."
TULI KUPFERBERG

Terry and Trish have been retired for ten years. They have done most of the things they set out to do in retirement. They have taken a couple of trips, got together with some long lost friends, spent time helping out their kids and grandkids and spent more time golfing and playing tennis. Terry and Trish are both in their early 70s and have seven beautiful grandchildren. Two of their children live in other provinces so they travel a couple of times a year to see them. Terry and Trish have been living their ideal retirement vision. But now, after ten years some cracks are beginning to appear.

They are concerned that they are getting into a rut. They are not unhappy with their current life; it just seems that they have been living the same year of life over and over again. It appears that this will continue for the foreseeable future unless they do something about it.

Even though they have been active up to now, it has become easier and easier to stay home due to fatigue and frankly, a lack of urgency. Since it is very easy to put off to tomorrow what could have been done today, Terry and Trish have both recognized they aren't as motivated to stay as active as they used to be. For the first time in many years they are both putting on weight. Is it time for a change? Should they think about getting involved in something different?

As they have become less active they are spending more time doing things on their own, rather than together. Over the past few months they have had more confrontations and conflicts than usual. They have also found that they are spending less time socializing with their friends. Their friends have all evolved and changed and they are finding that they just don't enjoy the time together with friends as much as they used to. Perhaps, it is time to think about meeting some new people? Yet, who wants to do so at this time in their life?

They want to "live the life they'd love to brag about", but are unsure of where to turn. They are looking for things they can be excited about. After ten good years, where do they go from here?

THE ISSUES

Terry and Trish have done the things they thought they'd always do in retirement, yet are left wanting more. They are in a rut that may begin to cause a rift in their relationship. They are becoming less active. They are becoming less social. They are becoming less stimulated and excited about their life. They are faced with a difficult, yet very common, question: will we continue to live the same year of life over and over again, or will we break the routine and try something different. Will they live one year of retirement 20 times over a 20 year period of retirement or will they continue to grow as people in an interesting and engaging manner?

Think about the following questions:

- Did your marriage last this long just because you are a really great companion… or did you have to work at it?

- Could you count on your next job promotion just because you showed up at work on time each day…or did you have to push yourself to go for more training or education?

- Do you have relationships with many different people just because you are someone that everyone else wants to be around…or did you have to work at maintaining those relationships?

- Do you have a great relationship with your kids and grandkids just because everyone loves to be with you…or did you have to make some sacrifices and make an extra effort for these relationships to grow and thrive?

- Are you fit and in good physical shape at this stage in your life because of your diet of coffee and pizza…or have you had to work hard on both your diet and your exercise?

You most certainly have had to work hard to obtain whatever was important to you in your life: the relationship with your spouse and children, your career advancements, relationships with friends and your health. Just because you are now retired, does this mean that you can coast for the next 20 years or does this mean that you may have to continue to work hard at a few things from time to time? Perhaps this will be even more difficult for you during this time due to your aging body? Perhaps you will have to work even harder for these things than you have had to in the past?

THE SOLUTIONS

In Chapter 6 we talked about the importance of creating a vision for your retirement. In Chapter 7 we talked about how to deal with many of the financial aspects related to the first two years of retirement and beyond.

Now we will spend more time dealing with the day to day realities of retirement. We want you to truly "live the life you'd love to brag about". This reinforces the principles mentioned in chapter 1. The Masters remain externally focused, they work together as a team with their spouse and they are always learning something new.

To be a Master, three things need to happen:

- **Focus on possibilities.** Focus on doing the little things well on a day to day basis. In the context of retirement planning, it is important to be acutely aware of the issues that need to be resolved, the things that need to be fixed, and the things you'd love to do, learn or improve.

- **Your purpose needs to be bigger than you.** Think in terms of your lasting legacy. A legacy is many things. It is your contribution to meaningful activities, it is the joy, memories and ideas that are left with others for years to come and it is also your financial contributions. Having a clearly defined legacy, for many people, is a very motivating, energizing and empowering aspect of their life.

- **Your relationships need to grow and evolve.** As time goes on and family roles change, relationships will change as well. Your relationship with others will change as their roles are evolving – a daughter becomes a mother, a son becomes a father.

These three steps are not exclusive to just retirement planning, but in planning for a healthy, happy and productive life.

Focus on the Possibilities

One of the ways for Terry and Trish to get out of the rut they are in today is to focus on a wide range of new possibilities. It will be these possibilities that will give them increased motivation, passion and energy in their day to day lives.

For example, in most people's lives, regardless of their stage in life, there are things to:

- Resolve
- Fix

- Do
- Learn
- Improve

As a matter of fact, you can make this into a game where the purpose of the game is:

- To push your personal boundaries
- To support your spouse in how they wish to push their own personal boundaries

Create a "Jar of Possibilities" that is filled with pieces of paper where each piece of paper contains a possibility. On each piece of paper is an item to Resolve, Fix, Do, Learn or Improve. It is something that the husband could add to on his own, or his spouse could add to on his behalf, and vice versa.

For example:

- **Things to resolve**: These are the unsolved problems with the important people in your life. Perhaps it is a broken relationship that needs mending, a conflict that should be addressed or a miscommunication that needs time for discussion. Address these issues today and over time you will be happier, healthier and more active. These unresolved issues can drain your energy and can cause you to become demoralized and isolated from family and friends. Resolving these unresolved issues will be like lifting a huge weight off your shoulders.

- **Things to fix**: Perhaps these are physical jobs around the house, or perhaps these are established and somewhat negative personality traits that you would like to change. As with most other things in life, when these issues remain unresolved, they can be a burden. Now that you are retired you have the time and ability to explore those things you'd love to fix.

- **Things to do**: Have you seen some of the museums or art galleries that are located in your area? Would you like to become more involved with local charities? Would you like to be more involved in coaching, teaching or certain sporting activities? What would you love to challenge your spouse to do in this area? Have you always wanted to write down the stories of your childhood or teach others how to paint?

- **Things to learn**: Keeping your mind active and challenged is extremely important in retirement. A healthy, active and vibrant mind can often translate into a healthy, active, and vibrant lifestyle. What is it that you always wanted to learn? Have you wanted to learn more about your family history, how to be a gourmet cook or play a musical instrument? Have you wanted to learn more about politics, gardening, woodworking or finance? Now is the time. A few hours a week and you can meet new people with similar interests.

- **Things to improve**: What would you love to do better? What would you like to challenge your spouse to do better? Would you like to improve your fitness, golf game, relationships with your grandchildren?

> *Challenge yourself to do more than just what may come naturally and you will "live the life you'd love to brag about".*

Without a plan, you may find that you are doing plenty of things, but none which are really challenging you in any way. What are the limits of your comfort zone and what do you need to do to push that comfort zone? This is what living a full and abundant life is all about.

The Jar of Possibilities Game in Action

Every Monday morning Terry and Trish set aside time to discuss specific topics under one of several important categories (resolve, fix, do, learn or improve).

For example, under the topic of resolving something, Terry and Trish have learned that the key to a boisterous retirement is to remove the obstacles to happiness. In Terry's case this meant resolving a troubled relationship that he had with his brother. Terry and Trish talked about what this issue meant to Terry and how it could be resolved. They developed a game plan and Trish has supported Terry every step along the way to help with this healing process. Today, Terry and his brother get together for a game of golf every couple of weeks. While their relationship is still a little tense at times, they are spending more time together than they ever have. This has been very energizing for Terry.

In another discussion, Trish needed to fix something – her lifetime habit of controlling the kids. While she was a natural and was very good at it, she soon realized that she needed to let go and change this behaviour. By developing a game plan, Trish has been able to reduce the level of stress in her life, and her children's lives, considerably. This has relieved the tension when the children visit and they have been dropping over more often.

One day Trish and Terry explored the topic of "doing something". They both wanted to give back and do something more for those less fortunate in their community. They had never had much time to volunteer when they were working and raising their family and it was very much outside of their comfort zone. However, they talked about this with other friends and found two other couples who volunteer weekly at a local soup kitchen. Now they do this together as a social outing that is enjoyable and helps them feel good about giving back to their community.

On another occasion Trish and Terry wrote down a number of different ideas that they thought would be fun to challenge the other person to "learn something new". They each wrote down 10 different ideas and put them into two different jars, one for Terry and one for Trish. The jars remain in the kitchen and are added to regularly throughout the month. At the beginning of each month they draw one piece of paper from their respective jar. During the month the challenge is to complete the task of learning the suggestion on the paper. In one instance Trish challenged Terry to get familiar with using e-mail. In another situation Terry challenged Trish to learn more about pairing wines with certain meals. A month later Trish challenged Terry to learn to barbecue three new fish dishes. In that same month Terry challenged Trish to spend more time learning how to paint, something that she has always wanted to do.

When the time came to discuss improvements, the conversation gravitated toward diet, health and exercise. Each has supported the other in setting and attaining small monthly goals related to their health, exercise, activity level and weight.

Terry and Trish have kept track of all of the things they have accomplished together since they began the Jar of Possibilities game. They also keep a list of all of the things they wish to discuss sometime in the future. This has been a fun, enlightening and empowering experience for both. They are energetic and active, both mentally and physically. This has lead to greater feelings of happiness and satisfaction and has also brought them closer together as a couple. They are a stronger team today than they have ever been.

Terry and Trish are "living the life they love to brag about" because they are constantly learning, improving their health, resolving outstanding issues, and spending time with the people they love. They know that their life today has no boundaries. They also know that they will always support each other in everything they do. They have overcome obstacles. They have examined their own fears and they have improved themselves.

Terry and Trish are mastering their life together. They have the time, freedom and flexibility to do so. As a matter of fact, they have also begun to share their knowledge and enthusiasm with others through a website that they have built together.

For Terry and Trish, "living the life they love to brag about" is not necessarily about spending more money, but evaluating how they spend their time.

Is this example realistic or is it just fantasy? Do you believe that once you have reached retirement that the relationship you have with your spouse is probably already entrenched and is not likely to change? Do you feel your spouse is capable of changing? Do you feel you or your spouse could benefit from dealing with some unresolved issues? Perhaps in a mischievous way, what would you love to challenge your spouse to do, to resolve, to learn about or to fix? How would you answer the same questions for yourself?

The Jar of Possibilities game is all about challenging yourself on a day to day basis. These challenges are meant to give you ideas, energy and optimism every day of your life.

In the same way that things like taxes, fees and inflation are key Killers of Wealth; complacency, a lack of exercise and failing to interact with others can be a key killer of your health, your relationships and, eventually, you.

Your Purpose Needs to be Bigger than You

At the end of the day, what will be your legacy? Your legacy may give you a great sense of purpose and passion throughout your retirement and may take you to places you have never dreamed of and it may introduce you to people that inspire you to achieve more.

A legacy may come in several different forms. It may be your contributions to an organization or cause. It may be the memories of joy and laughter with your children and grandchildren. It may be things that you write down and share with generations to come. Your legacy may also be a financial contribution. When you are considering your legacy, ask yourself these questions:

- When the retirement party is over, what type of legacy will you have from your work? For most people, despite the enjoyment experienced during their working years, after retirement, their contributions are often soon forgotten. Does your "life's work" need to be something more than just a life filled with work?

- Can money truly buy you happiness? Money can make things easier and it can also help to make problems disappear in the short run, but money can never truly buy you happiness.

- What are the greatest memories you have of your life? Are they the times when you played it safe, or when you made more money? Were they the times when you were with friends and family? Or perhaps they were the times when you went out of your comfort zone and lived to tell about it!

- In some cases, retired couples will begin to feel disillusioned early on in retirement. It is common for people to ask the question "Is this all there is to life?" Now that you've reached retirement, are you now just waiting to get sick and die?

Some people decide to take significant, yet well planned and calculated risks so as to really change the status quo. For some it may be travelling abroad for the first time. For some it may be volunteering in a soup kitchen or delivering Meals on Wheels. For some it may be writing their memoires. For some it may be learning a new activity or sport. For some it may be starting a home based business.

Remember, retirement is a truly unique time in life when you have a foundation of reliable income (that is non-work related). This foundation gives you choices and flexibility with how you spend your time. The greatest risk to a full retirement, and "living the life you'd love to brag about", is staying within your comfort zone.

With these questions in mind, Terry and Trish began to think more about their legacy and as a result began to explore the possibility of international humanitarian work. They researched the different possibilities and found that they could spend as much as two years away providing educational training and other assistance to people in impoverished nations. Terry and Trish decided to sell their home and structure their investments very conservatively.

After this experience Terry and Trish had a tremendous legacy of friendships, experiences and accomplishments that will benefit generations to come. They also documented their experiences in a book and, using an on-line book publishing service, produced copies for all family members. In the book are the stories of an incredible seven years living abroad and the lessons learned that Terry and Trish wished to pass on to their own grandchildren. Terry now volunteers to speak about their experiences to church groups and university classes throughout the year.

Perhaps your lasting legacy consists of:

- Volunteering your time as a Boy Scout leader.
- Working with children at a local school. Contact the school and offer to spend time over the lunch hour teaching a small group of kids about a topic you have an interest or skill in, such as woodworking, sporting activities, public speaking, nutrition, finances.
- Volunteering at a before school program serving breakfast to make sure kids are fed in the morning and ready to learn.
- Hosting exchange students from another country. This gives you the chance to meet young people from around the world.

These activities are examples of things you can do, from time to time throughout the year, that contribute to building your lasting legacy of memories, joy and wisdom.

Your legacy consists of the things you have done to enhance the world around you. This can be done through your actions as well as through your finances. You may find that your legacy projects give you great passion, meaning and inspiration.

Your Relationships Need to Grow and Evolve

As you move into retirement and perhaps grandparent mode, your role within the family changes. In some instances, these changes may create conflict. You need to be aware of the possibility of conflict.

For most people, family is everything. There is no greater joy than to see your children graduate from school, find a great spouse, marry and start a family. It is truly a miraculous, joyful and abundant time of life. Yet, one of the challenges during this time is to learn how to be a fabulous grandparent.

It is natural to want to provide wisdom, experience, support and encouragement to your children during this time. Yet, your children may not always be appreciative of your efforts or in agreement with your wisdom. You know from experience that over time your children have eventually appreciated your concerns, ideas and input, but you also know in most situations they have to learn life's lessons on their own.

In many situations grandparents are as emotionally attached to the grandchildren as are the parents. For the grandparent, the challenge is to know when to be there for support and when to step back and wait to be asked.

Many families cannot help but get into very deep and divided encounters when it comes to the grandchildren. Sometimes the grandparents, when the grandchildren are under their watchful eye, cannot help but contradict some of the values or beliefs of the parents. A strong and vocal grandparent, who has always been in a leadership role both in the family and in the outside world, cannot help but be a very vocal and opinionated grandparent. This may be the lifelong pattern of the relationship between what is now the grandparent and the parent and a pattern that probably needs to be broken if the relationships are to survive and grow.

The key to improving these relationships is in setting boundaries.

Physical Boundaries

- Separate residences are the ideal for grandparents and grandchildren. This gives the grandparents an opportunity to go home and "get a break" from the grandkids. It also creates the opportunity for the grandchildren to have a "sleepover" at the grandparent's house. Some of our greatest memories growing up have been the "one on one" time with our grandparents.

- By having this physical boundary it is easier for the parents to give in a little on the parenting issues. After all, what happens at grandma and grandpa's home is their business. However, the "behaviour expectations" at the child's home stand. This type of consistency and clarity is extremely important for the child to learn about boundaries. In some situations, it can be the opposite and the behaviour expectations are much greater when the children visit grandma and grandpa than when they are at home. It is substantially easier for the grandparent to be a grandparent when they are not physically living in the same premises. This physical boundary clearly distinguishes the role of the parents as the disciplinarians and the role of the grandparent as, well, the grandparent.

The Activity Related Boundaries

It is easy for the grandparent to do the laundry, clean the house, do the grocery shopping and prepare the meals while he/she is also looking after the grandchild. After all, the parents are away at work, weaving their way through the challenges and stresses of the day. Isn't this the least they could do to "help out"? Isn't this just being "nice"?

Absolutely, it is a very nice thing to do...from time to time. For some couples they may find that they are losing control of their own life when all of these things are being done for them. However, on occasion, as a surprise, the gesture is greatly appreciated.

Is the grandparent expected to discipline the grandchild? This may be something that the grandparent naturally gravitates to so as to maintain their own sanity. However, this may be in conflict with the values or approaches preferred by the parents. Naturally, there will be different views on parenting simply because the grandparents and the parents are from different generations. Also, since each of the parents was raised in a different manner, there is always a natural conflict that occurs between parents on what is right and wrong. It may take weeks, months or years for the parents to see eye to eye on certain parenting approaches. The grandparents' contribution to this may create greater confusion for the grandchild and frankly, may create additional conflict in the relationship between the parents.

Time is also an important boundary. If the grandchild spends more time with the grandparent than with the parent, it is natural for the child to see the grandparent as the "go to person" on most issues. This may deeply sadden the parents over time as they may find that they are missing out on the challenges, joys and frustrations of being a parent. This may create resentment and conflict between the children, the parents and the grandparents.

IN SUMMARY

The Healthy Years

No two retirements are alike. Even the questions surrounding one's retirement can be very different, even though the objectives are the same. To "do" retirement is one thing. To truly *Master Your Retirement* by "living the life you'd love to brag about" is something very different.

We want to challenge you to "take more risks", "take initiative", and "take action" on the things that you may not have considered before. If the goal is to "live the type of life you'd love to brag about" then perhaps this should be seen as your inspirational call to action. To truly *Master Your Retirement* is to challenge yourself, your spouse and the status quo; it is to build your lasting legacy of memories, joy and wisdom; and it is to enhance your relationships to a deeper level.

If these things are not in place, you will likely have some frustrations and challenges throughout your retirement.

Things You Need To Know

- It is very easy to get in a rut after just two or three years of retirement.

- It is easy to lose your energy and your focus when your goals and purpose are not clear.

- The Jar of Possibilities is a great way to keep things lively and interesting, both personally, and within your marriage/partnership relationship.

- A clearly defined lasting legacy is an amazing motivator and energizer. A lasting legacy can be many things including your contribution to a meaningful cause, the sharing of insight and wisdom, writing down the family stories, sharing laughter and fun with family and friends as well as lasting financial gifts.

- Relationships with your children and grandchildren will change and evolve over the years. It is important to recognize how you should adapt to these changes so that your relationships will continue to grow.

Questions You Need To Ask

- Am I in a rut today? Do I need to try something new or shake things up? Is the same true for my spouse?

- If you could challenge your spouse to do one thing, what would that be?

- If you could take one risk over the next 12 months, what would you do?

- What do you want to be known for? How do you want others to remember you?

- Are you living out the vision you have of your lasting legacy?
- If you could do one thing over the next 12 months to enhance your lasting legacy, what would you do?
- Are you concerned about one or more specific relationship with your children or grandchildren? What do you feel you need to do to enhance that relationship?

Things You Need To Do

- Find a jar. Label it "Jar of Possibilities". Cut up pieces up paper, put ideas on the papers, and put the papers inside the jar. Put the jar in a prominent location in your home so that you will see it throughout each day.
- Every Monday morning sit down and draw one item from the jar. Focus on that one item over the next one to two weeks.
- Think about those people (past or present) whom you really admire. What is it that you admire about them?
- Think about a cause or a mission that is bigger than you are. Talk about this with your spouse and friends. What is it? Perhaps this is something that you can do together with others.
- Read books about grandparenting.
- Be supportive of your children and keep the dialogue open.

Decisions You Need To Make

- What will be my lasting legacy?
- What would I like to learn?
- What can I improve?
- How can I be a better parent? Grandparent?

Mastery Principle

Challenge yourself each and every day to learn something new. Retirement will never get boring, that's for sure. Be externally focused, work as a team with your spouse and never stop learning.

CHAPTER

9

When Illness Strikes

"Outstanding people have one thing in common: an absolute sense of mission." ZIG ZIGLAR

Lawrence and Linda are 75 years old. While they are both very healthy and active themselves, not a month goes by where they don't hear about someone they know falling ill or battling some form of health ailment. This is a common conversation among their peers.

They are doing everything they can to remain active, eat well, take vitamin supplements and see their physician regularly. Yet, they want to make sure that they are prepared in advance for a day when one of them may fall ill.

They are unsure of the full impact of an illness. What if the person who falls ill is the one who normally pays the bills and looks after the finances? How will they adapt?

What if the person who falls ill needs to receive long term care or move into a long term care facility? How will this impact their income and lifestyle?

Will they have enough income to support their medical needs? What other sources of income could they draw from?

Lawrence and Linda want to make sure they are ready for when an illness strikes. But they are unsure of what to do and how to go about doing it.

THE ISSUES

Recent statistics suggest that older Canadians in general are living healthy lives in their later years. However, age-related restrictions to life activities affect one in five seniors aged 65 to 74, just under one in three between 75 and 85 and one half of seniors aged 85 or more.

While there has been a noticeable decline in mortality from heart disease and strokes, cancer and respiratory diseases have increased. In addition, while women live longer than men, approximately two thirds of these extra years are spent living with a disability.

The vast majority of seniors take medication, stay in hospital longer and require the services of care giving (either informal or formal) for some portion of their later years.

The number one issue related to aging is the cost of long term care. Long term care facilities charge as much as $70 per day. Though the cost of long term care is subsidized by provincial governments, the resident is responsible for a portion of the cost. The long term care fee charged by the government is dependent upon the total gross income for both spouses. On the one hand you may feel that $70 per day is quite inexpensive given the treatment, meals and services provided. Yet, $70 per day is also equal to $25,550 for the year. The number one issue and risk to a couple in retirement is the ability to fund this expense while also maintaining the current home and lifestyle of the healthy spouse. In effect, when illness strikes, you may be funding the cost of two homes at the same time. The average length of stay in a long term care facility is three to five years. This could be a considerable expense for most families.

This chapter turns our attention to Master Principle 5: Anticipate future risks. It is inevitable that illness will strike one or both spouses at some point in time. The Masters will be ready for this, but will you?

THE SOLUTIONS

You may find yourself in one of two different health related situations:

- The need for treatment: if you have just had a heart attack, stroke and or been diagnosed with cancer and need immediate treatment, or
- The need for long term care: when you require assistance with daily living over a longer period of time.

In each of these situations there is a need for diagnosis, treatment and cash. Some of the cash may come from your investments, assets or insurance while some may come from your tax return. Each of these options is described below.

In addition to this, there also needs to be clear instructions to those around you of how you wish your affairs to be handled. This is the legal aspect of handling an illness. At the end of the chapter we discuss briefly the importance of having a Will, a Power of Attorney and a Living Will.

Finally, to prepare for such a situation, some steps will be outlined at the end of this chapter to help you measure the impact of such an illness or long term care need.

The Need for Treatment

There are several important financial issues to be aware of as it relates to treatment.

Costs of Treatment

In Canada, most of the costs related to treatment will be paid for by the Provincial Government. However, you may find that the waiting time for treatment may be too long for your personal preference. In this instance you may wish to receive treatment outside of Canada. The cost of such treatment may range from $20,000 to $200,000. The cost for on-going medication may be as much as $2,000 per month and the cost for home renovations or the purchase of necessary medical equipment at home may also be significant.

It is also important to note that in the most recent Federal Budgets, the tax deductibility of certain medical treatments has been taken away. In an environment of a slower growth economy, potentially rising interest rates and inflation combined with an aging demographic, one can only assume that the type of health care benefits available in the future will be less, or much less, than what we are accustomed to today.

Treatment Funding Options

There are several ways in which you can plan for these expenses in advance:

- **Critical Illness Insurance**: Critical Illness Insurance is designed to pay you a lump sum, tax-free benefit in the event you are diagnosed with a critical illness and you survive for a period of 30 days after the diagnosis. The most common critical illnesses relate to a heart attack, stroke and cancer. The amount of benefit you receive is based on the amount you choose at the time of application. However, many group insurance programs now provide a basic flat amount of coverage as part of the overall group program. If you must choose the amount of coverage, choose an amount that is equal to approximately one year of before tax income. Critical illness insurance may allow you to seek the most appropriate treatment, in a timely manner and at the most appropriate location. The insurance is best purchased when you are younger as the cost of the premiums increase with age. Typically, coverage is available up to the age of 75.

- **International Health Insurance**: Some health insurance products currently available in Canada provide funding for medical treatments abroad. The funding will also cover transportation and hotel costs for family. This type of coverage is ideal for busy entrepreneurs, executives and their families.

- **Investments:** You can cash in some of your investments to pay for this treatment. Remember, if you cash in your RRSP investments you may find that your total taxable income now violates the "OAS Clawback Zone" which means you will pay a considerable amount of tax and clawback to fund this need and you will likely place a substantial dent in your RRSP portfolio.

  Cashing in some of your non-registered investments will also deplete this source of capital and may eliminate its ability to generate future income. Cashing in your investments is an option, but it is less than ideal.

- **Taking a Loan:** You can borrow money to pay for medical needs or complete home adaptations now needed as a result of the illness. This can be a good approach to protect your investment capital. The loan can be rolled into your mortgage so that you can pay it off over a long period of time. Many provinces provide grants and/or low-interest loans to cover the cost of home adaptations. Converting a portion of your investments into an annuity will enable you to receive a higher monthly income that is guaranteed for life. The higher income can help to make the monthly loan payment.

- **Tax Benefits:** There are several tax benefits available to you when medical treatment is required including home renovation costs, moving expenses related to a move to a more accessible dwelling, expenses related to travel to receive medical service and expenses paid for medical benefits. These benefits are always being adjusted at both the provincial and federal government level. Many of the disability related tax credits and tax credits for medical expenses have been expanded in recent years. However, remember that these are tax credits whereby the credit is multiplied by a basic federal tax rate of 15% and is then applied against taxes payable.

The Need for Long Term Care

A significant financial risk to every family happens when one spouse enters a care facility while the other stays at home. Now you are covering the cost of two homes. If this happens early in retirement, 10 or more years of home or facility care expenses can place considerable financial hardship on the healthy spouse. It is important for the retired couple to understand these risks and to consider the burden and stress it can place on the entire family. The extended family will need to consider ways in which they can support the couple while the aging couple may wish to set out their instructions in advance to give guidance on these challenging and highly emotional issues.

Long Term Care Funding Options

- **Long Term Care Insurance:** This type of insurance provides a monthly tax-free income of your choosing at the time of application. When you purchase long term care insurance you are purchasing a specific "daily" amount of benefit. For example, you may wish to consider $50, $75, $100, $200 or more of daily benefit. The plan is best purchased before you retire. The benefits are payable for a certain period of time or for life. When choosing long term care insurance you can opt for home care, facility care or both types of coverage. As you can see from the example at the beginning of the chapter, an additional $75 per day would be extremely beneficial to cover those long term costs.

The cost of long term care insurance is reasonably expensive and it is difficult to know if you should insure both spouses or just one. Insuring both spouses with long term care coverage is beneficial but expensive. If you were to insure only the husband, the healthy wife is now guaranteed to have enough money to continue to stay in her current home. Alternatively, if you were to insure only the wife, this may provide the wife, who is expected to outlive the husband in most cases, with long term financial security.

Some insurance companies are beginning to offer "first to claim" coverage whereby both spouses are part of the plan, but the benefit is paid to only the first individual who claims. This is an excellent product choice because you are covering the risk of both spouses yet only paying for one. In fact, the actual premium works out to be 10% to 15% less than the cost of two individual plans.

As with most forms of insurance, you are insuring the risk of incurring significant financial hardship. However, you never know if this is something that will impact you or not. The money may be really well spent or you may find that you never claim on this product and thus do not feel that you have received good value for your money invested into this product.

In some instances, if you do not make a long term care claim, some portion of your premiums paid can come back to you as a "return of premium" benefit.

- **Joint Last Survivor Insurance**: A flexible long term solution is a Joint Last Survivor Insurance Policy, as you are guaranteed to eventually receive the insurance payout. The death benefit is paid on the last death.

The premiums on this type of life insurance are substantially less than individual life insurance coverage.

There are several benefits to this approach.

- Death benefit proceeds can be set up to by-pass your estate and go directly to your beneficiaries. The money received by your beneficiaries is then tax-free.

- You always know how much life insurance will be payable to your beneficiaries.

- If you know that your heirs are to receive this Joint Last Survivor life insurance benefit, then you may feel more comfortable drawing income from your investments, knowing you are still leaving a substantial legacy for your heirs.

- **Impaired Annuity**: An annuity is identical to a pension plan. A lump sum of money is given to an insurance company which in turn guarantees to pay a monthly income for life. An "impaired" annuity provides a higher level of monthly income due to "less than standard health". If, due to your current health, your life expectancy is shorter than normal, the insurance company will take this into account when calculating the amount of monthly benefit provided to you. In the event that one spouse enters a long term care facility and there is a need to generate more income from investments, an impaired annuity may be an excellent solution for lifetime, guaranteed income.

- **Involuntary Separation**: An "involuntary separation" occurs when one spouse enters a long term care facility; this move was not a choice, but a necessity. When this occurs, the other spouse can apply to have any income tested benefits calculated on a single income basis. Declaring an involuntary separation could lessen the amount of the OAS clawback. Talk with your tax professional to find the best solution for your situation. For more information on involuntary separation, contact your local Service Canada office.

Long Term Care Related Tax Benefits

There are several important tax credits to be aware of:

- **Caregiver Tax Credit**: If you support and live with an infirm dependant in a home which you maintain, you may claim a specified amount for that dependant as a non-refundable credit against taxes payable.

  To qualify, the dependant must meet these three criteria: a) be at least 18 years old, b) be either the child or grandchild of the taxpayer or the taxpayer's spouse or common-law partner, or the parent, grandparent, brother, sister, uncle, aunt, niece or nephew of the taxpayer or the taxpayer's spouse or common-law partner and resident in Canada at any time in the year, and c) be either the taxpayer's parent or grandparent and at least 65 years old or dependent on the taxpayer because of mental or physical infirmity

- **Infirm Adult Tax Credit**: If you support a dependant who is at least 18 years of age and dependent on you because of mental or physical infirmity, you may claim a non-refundable credit against taxes payable. To qualify, the dependant must be your child or grandchild (or child or grandchild of your spouse or common-law partner, or the parent, grandparent, brother, sister, uncle, aunt, niece or nephew of the taxpayer or the taxpayer's spouse or common-law partner and resident in Canada at any time in the year). Note that you cannot claim both the Caregiver Credit and the Infirm Adult Credit at the same time.

Your Legal Affairs

Three important steps should be considered with regards to your personal affairs. Is your Will up to date? Do you have a Power of Attorney? Have you completed a Living Will (health care directive)?

- **Last Will and Testament**: This legal document tells the world who will look after your affairs after you die, and to whom your assets are to flow. This can be a very simple document or it can be extremely complex, depending on your personal situation. It is recommended you see a lawyer to prepare your will to ensure your requests will be carried out as you intended.

- **Power of Attorney**: This document states the name, obligations and responsibilities of the person who will look after your affairs in the event you are not able to do so for yourself. Typically, this is a situation where you are unable to pay your own bills, look after your own investments or make your own financial decisions due to incapacity or illness.

- **The Living Will (Health Care Directive)**: This document describes your wishes regarding the type of treatment you are to receive in the event that you may be suffering from a long illness, in great pain and are unlikely to recover. This is a very helpful document to your family, letting them know in advance your wishes in the event that such a situation may arise. This document can alleviate the need for caregivers and/or family members to struggle with difficult decisions during a time of extreme stress. The instructions on a Living Will should be clear and easily understood by medical personnel. It is recommended you speak with your doctor before you complete your Living Will.

How do These Options Relate to Your Overall Financial Plan and the Great Killers of Wealth?

It is without dispute that health care costs are rising at a considerable rate. This is referred to as health care inflation. Many commentators refer to this as one of the great risks related to retirement and thus suggest the purchase of things such as long term care insurance to offset this risk and to provide more choices.

The challenge, as I see it, is that this approach means that you need to take money from your budget today to provide future funding for an event that may or may not happen, or that may happen for only a short period of time. Since the cost of funding such a plan is quite expensive, you are faced with a choice of either cutting back on your lifestyle desires, cutting expenses in other areas, drawing more income from your portfolio, or taking more risk in your portfolio to offset these costs. The first two options (cutting lifestyle, reducing expenses) may encroach on things that are the highest priority in your life, so this may not be a good option.

Alternatively, drawing more income from your portfolio or taking more portfolio risk may then put your portfolio at risk from significant market volatility and thus put your savings at greater risk. Again, not something that I'd typically encourage one to do.

So what is one to do? Having "dignity" in the final years of life is one of life's most important goals and benefits. In a nutshell, aging is for the birds. Your mind is alert but your body betrays you. Therefore, giving yourself the option to maximize your dignity in your final years is an important goal for many.

As discussed in this chapter, several things can be done:

- Sell your home and use the tax free proceeds to fund a higher quality life in a senior care facility.
- Borrow from the equity in your home to meet your funding needs.
- Convert some of the RRSP or investments into an annuity or an impaired annuity so as to generate more income without the risk of taking on more market volatility.
- Purchase a joint last survivor life insurance plan. The cost to fund such a plan will be similar to that of a long term care insurance plan. The only difference is that the life insurance plan has a 100% probability of paying out. In the event that additional debts are incurred to fund these needs, either by the couple or by family members, the insurance can make it all right by creating enough new money (i.e.: the life insurance death benefit) to pay all of these expenses back.

IN SUMMARY

When Illness Strikes

To assess your ability to survive an unexpected illness or long term care need, consider the following:

Things You Need To Know

- Both a short term illness and a long term care need can be a substantial expense.
- Specific insurance products can be purchased to pay for medical expenses.
- Tax deductions and tax credits may be available to offset the cost of medical expenses.
- A substantial financial risk you face is the need for long term care assistance for a long period of time, while the healthy spouse lives in your current home. The cost of financing two "homes" can be considerable.

Questions You Need To Ask

- What is the financial risk to you?
- What sources of capital could you draw on to cover these expenses?
- Is there a shortfall? Would you feel more comfortable having part of the risk insured?
- Are you claiming all available expenses and credits?
- How will an illness impact the healthy spouse? Will the healthy spouse require assistance with the finances?

Things You Need To Do

- Update your Will.
- Prepare a Power of Attorney and Living Will.
- Discuss the Will, Power of Attorney and Living Will with your children so that everyone is aware of your wishes.
- Prepare a financial analysis noting the impact to the healthy spouse in the event the other spouse enters a long term care facility.
- Decide if you would feel more comfortable with the purchase of long term care insurance.

Decisions You Need To Make

- Is preparing for this Phase in advance of benefit to my spouse and me?

Mastery Principle

The key to success comes from preparation for both the expected and unexpected events. We know that illness will strike, often at the most unexpected time. The extent to which we are prepared will enable us to focus on the health needs of the ill, rather than our financial needs, regardless of the outcome. Be detail oriented, manage the risks and be forward-looking.

10

Being on Your Own

"Paint a masterpiece daily. Always autograph your work with excellence." GREG HICKMAN

Theresa and Don held hands waiting for Dr. Smith to give them the results of the tests. Don had been receiving cancer treatments for two years now, but he was growing weaker and weaker as time wore on. Don had been in the hospital now for almost six months. Unfortunately, the news was not good and there was nothing more the doctors could do for Don. It was just a matter of time.

Don is 75 and Theresa is 74. Both had been quite active up until two years ago when the first diagnosis was made. They both remained focused on Don's health, never daring to think that he may pass away before his time. But now it was a different story, the unthinkable was about to happen.

As the shock of the news set in for Theresa, a greater fear also took over her thoughts. She didn't know very much about their household finances, his pension, their investments or their taxes. Don had always taken care of their finances. All of their children were grown, married and living in other provinces. Who should she talk to? Who could she count on for help? Would she have enough money? How would she spend her time? What would she do?

Not only was she devastated to lose her lifelong partner, but she was also sad about the unfulfilled dreams they shared together. They had so many plans that now would never come to pass. She was also terrified of making the wrong decision regarding their finances. Theresa was really scared.

THE ISSUES

There are many important financial issues that arise when one spouse survives the other:

- How much income will you have after your spouse passes away?
- What are your new monthly expenses?
- Will you have enough income to live on?
- Is this income safe and secure?
- Where is the cheque book, the bank accounts and the tax forms?
- When do you file the tax returns and who looks after this?
- Who is looking after your investments?
- Where are the Wills?
- Do you have enough money to pay for a proper funeral?

There are also many important softer issues that arise. Many of these will depend on the age of the surviving spouse:

- How will you spend your time?
- Who will you spend your time with?
- Who can you talk to about your grief and sadness?
- What should you do with the cottage?
- What should you do with the family home?
- What do you need to do to feel safe?

While the questions may appear to be complex, the answers are quite simple. You need to take a deep breath, gain control, tie up loose ends and then begin to plan ahead for the future.

While it is always difficult to be truly ready for such a day, anticipating what may need to be done at that time can often encourage people to take steps today so as to make things easier for the surviving spouse. Again, we wish to anticipate the issues that may arise at that time, be detail oriented and forward-looking.

THE SOLUTIONS

After the funeral, the surviving spouse can often be faced with a tidal wave of issues, questions and decisions. At a time when you may wish to just sit back, reflect, remember and grieve in the quiet and comfort of your own home, many important issues need to be discussed. It is also possible that the surviving spouse is meeting his/her advisors for the first time, or for the first time in many years.

The best approach is to identify the priorities and do a few things at a time. Each of these priorities can be broken down into three distinct areas: gain control, tie up loose ends and plan for the future.

Gain Control

Great comfort and peace of mind will come from a basic understanding of where you stand financially. To gain control means that you have control over your bank accounts, your expenses and your income and you have an understanding of where they are, how much they are and the amount of money you have to spend each month.

If your bank accounts are "jointly held" between both spouses, there are no issues of concern. You can continue to write cheques and pay bills from this account. However, if one or more accounts were in the name of the deceased spouse, these accounts must be identified and transferred to an account in the name of the surviving spouse. To do this, speak to your local bank branch, they will help you with this process.

To avoid difficult situations with bank accounts, ensure that all accounts are jointly held with rights of survivorship.

Make a list of your monthly expenses. Look at the last two to three months of bank statements to see which expenses are automatically drawn from your account and which expenses had been paid for by cheque or credit card each month. Many people keep excellent records in their cheque book and this can be another great place to look when sizing up the monthly expenses. Watch the incoming mail very closely for overdue notices of payment. By paying close attention to the incoming mail you will begin to gain an understanding of your monthly expenses.

Now that you are on your own, it is important to identify
your income sources and any changes to that income
as a result of the loss of your partner.

Pension Plan

Prior to Don's death, he was receiving a Canada Pension Plan (CPP) monthly income benefit. After his death, his surviving spouse will no longer receive this income. Instead, in its place, will be a survivor's monthly income benefit. In general, the total maximum amount that the surviving spouse will receive from the Canada Pension Plan is equal to the maximum monthly income benefit available at that time. Therefore, the maximum amount of survivor pension received will be (approximately) the difference between the maximum benefit available and the current benefits received by the surviving spouse from their own Canada Pension Plan retirement benefit amount. For most surviving spouses, this will mean that the total CPP monthly income benefit will likely decrease.

You must notify the Canada Pension Plan of the death of your spouse through one of the Service Canada offices in your area. When you do, you will also complete an application for a "Lump Sum Death Benefit" that will pay you a one time payment of $2,500.

Old Age Security

If, prior to Don's death, Don was receiving over $500 per month in Old Age Security income, then Theresa will see a reduction of over $6000 of annual income.

Employer Pension Plan

If Don had a pension plan with a previous employer(s), the monthly income benefit on this plan may be reduced by approximately 33% to 50%. You must notify the employer of the passing of your spouse. They will advise you of the amount of pension income that you will receive from this point forward. You can certainly review this information in advance so as to assist you with your long term plans.

Annuity Income

An annuity is similar to a pension plan and may also be reduced by as much as 33% to 50%. Notify the insurance company of the passing of your spouse and they will notify you of the amount of annuity income you will receive from this point forward. Ideally, any annuity that you set up yourself should provide 100% of the income to the surviving spouse.

RRIF and Other Investments

As with the bank accounts, you must convert the ownership of these investments to the name of the surviving spouse. In many instances you can combine the RRIFs and have one or two large accounts rather than several small accounts. Your investment advisor or a representative from each company can provide you with the necessary documents to complete these changes.

In many instances these accounts will be jointly owned with rights of survivorship. This means that the account will continue on as is without any difficulties. You will, however, need to change the ownership of the investment to the surviving spouse in due course.

Note: In January of each year you will receive an annual investment statement from any company holding your investments. Watch your mail closely during this time to make sure you haven't missed changing ownership of any of your investments.

Life Insurance Proceeds

It is a top priority to apply for any life insurance proceeds that are payable to you. Contact your insurance advisor to assist you with this or speak directly with the insurance company. In most cases, they will need a copy of the funeral director's death certificate to process the claim.

Note: There may be life insurance protection on your loans, mortgages and even your credit cards. It is important to apply for all such payments IF this type of coverage is already in place. In general, we have found the cost for such coverage to be quite expensive and do not typically encourage people to take out this coverage.

> *By taking control over your bank accounts, your income and your expenses, you now have control over your personal finances. You will begin to see whether you have enough income to cover your monthly expenses.*

At this stage, you have gained control over your financial affairs, but not made any significant changes or decisions. Before making any decisions, you will need to probate the Will of the deceased spouse. Probating the Will is done with the assistance of a lawyer. Probating a Will is the formal process to ensure the Last Will and Testament of a deceased individual is fulfilled according to the terms and conditions of the Will and the local provincial court certifies the process. This may take several weeks or months to complete. Once the court has approved the probated Will the financial institutions may require a copy for their records to proceed with changing the ownership of the RRIF and other investment assets to the name of the surviving spouse.

Some financial institutions will proceed with changing the ownership of the investments from one spouse to another if they are provided a copy of the death certificate and the beneficiaries all sign a form that releases the financial institution from any liability. Contact your financial institution to check on the documents required.

There are ways to prepare for this situation in advance and relieve the stress for the surviving spouse:

- Convert your assets (home, non-registered investment account and bank accounts) to joint ownership today.
- Know in advance the changes that will occur to pension plans and annuities on the death of either spouse.
- Prepare a monthly budget and share it with your spouse.

- Prepare a list of all bank and investment accounts.
- Prepare a list of advisors and who should be contacted for each area of knowledge.
- Tell your spouse and Executor the location of your Will.
- Discuss these implications with your children so that everyone knows the overall game plan.

Unfortunately, some adult children prey on the lone surviving parent to help them through a financial crisis or to support them in their next business endeavour. In many cases, a surviving spouse may feel lonely and vulnerable and can be easily manipulated or pushed to lend or give money to this child. The other siblings may not be aware of what is happening until they realize their brother or sister has depleted a large portion of their father/mother's investment capital. Not only will this impact the surviving spouse's standard of living, but will also impact the inheritance for the others – then the sparks really begin to fly.

To avoid such a situation, some or all of the assets could be left to the surviving spouse in a "Spousal Trust". By doing so, the surviving spouse would receive income from the trust but no capital could be withdrawn (unless specifically provided for in the trust deed).

If you, as the surviving spouse, feel uncomfortable or threatened by a family member asking you for a loan or gift of money, tell someone. Tell other family members, friends or a professional such as a bank employee, social worker or law enforcement professional. Remember, you are not only protecting your income, but also the legacy you will leave to your family and/or community.

Tie Up Loose Ends

There are many financial issues that need to be dealt with, but not all are necessarily urgent and can wait until you have completed the first steps discussed previously.

Real Estate Ownership

The ownership of your real estate must be changed to the name of the surviving spouse. This includes your home, your cottage, vacation home and any other properties. If the property is jointly owned you will remain an owner of the property and have rights to make decisions about the property. However, for greater clarity you will want to change the ownership to the name of the surviving spouse within a reasonable period of time.

Cars

Do you need to insure and operate two cars? Does it make sense to sell one car and thus stop the monthly insurance payment? The sooner you do this the better, but this is not an urgent issue.

Credit Cards

Cancel all credit cards in the name of the deceased spouse. But before you do so, check to see if there is any life insurance or accidental death insurance coverage on any outstanding balance.

Memberships

Cancel the annual membership to various clubs that the deceased spouse enjoyed on their own. If you also attend the same club, you may not need to make any changes until it is time to renew the memberships.

Subscriptions

Cancel magazine or other subscriptions that do not interest you.

Medical Insurance

Cancel coverage for deceased spouse.

Plan for Your Future

Planning for the future may not take place for a year or even two years after the death of the spouse. Of course, the sooner it is done the better, but the surviving spouse may not be ready to take these steps until they have had a chance to work through their grief. Making big decisions while in the grieving period can be extremely stressful. This may result in feelings of making the wrong decision because you felt rushed or confused at the time. It is always best to let things settle down first before taking on significant decisions.

It is now time to review your retirement vision and your retirement income plan. You have experienced a significant life changing event which will affect your plans for the future. Follow the processes described in this book and revisit your plan every three to five years.

Assess Your Taxes

As discussed in the previous chapters, you need to know if your income is moving into higher tax brackets or higher clawback levels. If your income is entering these levels consider ways to reduce your total taxable income. When considering how to do this, the first step will be to review your income and expenses.

IN SUMMARY

Being On Your Own

This book is about Mastering Your Retirement. To *Master Your Retirement* we recognize that there are several phases that you will go through during your retirement years. If you know in advance what these phases will look like, you can do some very important pro-active planning. It is clear that one day one spouse will be gone and one will survive. If the surviving spouse knows about all the important issues in advance it can make life, at this most difficult time, as calm and assured as possible.

While your children were young, you often encouraged them to "clean up their mess". The same is true for adults. One such "mess" relates to your investments, real estate, Wills, and finances. If you "clean up the mess" for your surviving spouse, he/she will continue on with life without encountering financial obstacles or surprises.

THINGS YOU NEED TO KNOW

- When one spouse passes away, your household income may decrease.
- CPP may be reduced.
- The deceased's OAS benefit will stop.
- Annuity income or pension plan income may also be reduced.
- Know in advance how the death of a spouse will affect the financial picture of the survivor.

QUESTIONS YOU NEED TO ASK

- Which assets are jointly owned and which assets are not jointly owned?
- Are the assets that are jointly owned referred to as "tenants in common" or "joint tenants with rights of survivorship"? These two descriptions mean two different things. The latter option is the most preferred.
- Are all bank accounts, investment accounts and insurance policies listed in one location?
- Where is the Will?
- Is there a list of all advisors and their roles?

THINGS YOU NEED TO DO

- Take a moment to "analyze" the financial future of the surviving spouse. To do so, assume that one spouse has passed away and the surviving spouse is on their own. What decisions will they have to make? What information will they need?

- Plan your funeral arrangements in advance.
- Discuss and share your plans with your children so that everyone knows the game plan.
- If there is a risk of the surviving spouse being taken advantage of by an unscrupulous family member(s), consider putting most or all assets into a "Spousal Trust".

DECISIONS YOU NEED TO MAKE

- Is it important to you to prepare for this next phase in advance, for the benefit of you and your spouse?
- Is it necessary to share your plans with your children so that everyone knows the "game plan"?

Mastery Principle

The alone years can be a time when the surviving spouse feels very vulnerable. Preparing in advance, and sharing this game plan with all family members, will help to create comfort with the surviving spouse and certainty with all family members. Be detail oriented, anticipate the risks and be forward-looking.

11

Your Final Estate Plan

*"When it's all over, it's not who you were. It's whether
you made a difference."* BOB DOLE

A week after the funeral, the family gathered to read Mary's last Will and Testament. Mary had lived a long and gracious life, given back to her community in many ways and played an active role in the lives of her children and grand-children. While the family was naturally sad, they also admired the life that Mary and her husband Bill had lived. But what really impressed the family the most was the lasting legacy they left behind. Bill, Mary's husband, had passed away a year earlier.

Mary's total estate value was just over $2 million. This was very significant for the modest life and income that she and Bill had throughout their life together. It was also amazing to see that much of this money would be going to the beneficiaries tax-free.

The family knew that considerable planning had always taken place and both their father and their mother wanted to make sure that the taxes were minimized in their estate. Each family member would receive a significant inheritance while also giving a generous amount of money to charity.

Bill and Mary always enjoyed their life, and the decisions they made along the way were highly influenced by their legacy desires. They both felt very strongly about leaving this world a better place in some small way – and they did.

THE ISSUES

How do you find the right balance between meeting today's income needs while planning for tax efficiency and greater estate benefits down the road?

The answer to this question is "good planning". You need to know which assets will generate tax in your estate and which assets will not. Your objective is to gravitate towards the tax-free assets and move away from those that are less tax efficient.

What can you do to enhance your legacy to your family and community? What can you do to leave the world a better place?

This can be achieved in several ways, many of which are not necessarily financially related. Your legacy may be your time and commitment to a particular cause in the community. Perhaps you are already planning on leaving a financial donation to this cause. To multiply your legacy you may wish to consider the use of life insurance.

Have you chosen your beneficiaries wisely? In many cases the tax department is the largest single beneficiary of your estate. The estate could pay 30% to 40% of the value of the estate in taxes unless a) you are able to accumulate more tax-free assets or b) pay the taxes that are due with fewer dollars. Are you aware of all you can do to make this happen? After all, why wouldn't you want to do this? Why would you purposely leave more money to the government than any other beneficiary?

When planning your legacy you want to make sure you "begin with the end in mind." By planning ahead and focusing on the final outcomes you can make sure you make appropriate decisions along the way.

Now let's take a look at how Bill and Mary's story evolved.

THE SOLUTIONS

Bill and Mary's family home was valued at $500,000. The home is tax-free because the house was classified as their principal residence under the Income Tax Act. Bill and Mary also purchased a joint last survivor life insurance policy for $1 million close to 15 years ago; the proceeds of this policy are passed on to the heirs tax-free. The remaining value is the investment portfolio. Much of this value was held in the Tax-Free Savings Account they opened in 2009. Over the past 15 years they have diligently deposited the maximum of $10,000 ($5,000 per person) a year into this plan. The principal investment as well as the interest on this investment money is received tax-free into the estate.

Fifteen years ago Bill and Mary found a way to multiply the value of their estate. They were planning all along to leave $200,000 of their estate to charity. However, they found that they could now use this same $200,000 to purchase a $1 million life insurance policy and triple the value of their legacy. They decided to leave $100,000 to six different charitable organizations that included helping the poor, medical research, education grants and their church.

Bill and Mary also decided to leave $600,000 to each of their two children in the form of a testamentary trust. The income inside the testamentary trust is taxed similar to an individual taxpayer. This will help save thousands of dollars in tax over the remaining lives of their children as well as their grandchildren. Note: these rules are currently under review by the Department of Finance.

If Bill and Mary had done nothing to plan for their final transition, their estate would be subject to several hundred thousand dollars in additional taxes and they would have had less money to share. Bill and Mary were able to triple the amount of money they would give to charity as well as double the amount of money they would give to their children and grandchildren.

Bill and Mary's lasting legacy was substantial:

- Additional income and financial resources for their children.
- Additional resources for important community projects and charities for today and years to come.
- The memories and laughter they shared throughout their life with their children and grandchildren.
- Over the past 10 years Bill and Mary collaborated in writing a book about their lives, their family history, the lessons they learned and the wisdom they gained. This book was presented to the family at the time the Will was read.

Enhancing Your Personal Legacy

Peace of mind and happiness is derived from a sense of satisfaction, satisfaction of a job well done or a life well lived. Satisfaction comes from knowing that you took some risks along the way, you always did your best, your relationships were healthy and loving and, in some small way, the world is a better place today because of you.

Your legacy is not just a financial legacy. Your legacy may be your children and grandchildren, the volunteer work you've done in the community, the contributions you've made to make the community a better place, the time spent coaching other children and adults and the memories and the laughter shared.

What are the activities that give you the most satisfaction? How could you enhance your satisfaction?

- Would you set up a scholarship fund for your favorite academic pursuit?
- Would you volunteer to spend your time with children?
- Would you write a book describing your experiences when travelling abroad?

- Would you spend more time visiting with family and friends?

- Would you volunteer your time at the local food bank; would you deliver Meals on Wheels?

- Would you dedicate more time and energy to those in our society who are less fortunate?

- Would you spend more time learning something new?

- Would you spend time getting the work of others acknowledged? Perhaps there is someone you know who should be included in your local sports hall of fame?

There are so many things that one can do to enhance their personal legacy. Enhancing your personal legacy is about enhancing your personal sense of satisfaction and making the world a better place. What would you like to do today, to increase your sense of satisfaction and enhance the world around you? This is the heart and soul of your lasting legacy!

Take a moment now and start making a list of all the things that are important to you. How can you multiply the benefit or outcome of these things? With these thoughts in mind, what do you feel could be your lasting legacy?

Have You Chosen Your Beneficiaries Wisely?

Whether you like it or not, the tax department will be one of the beneficiaries of your estate. It is your choice where your money goes when you die. Do you want to do everything you can to minimize the tax payable?

Taxable Assets

- **RRIF/RRSP investments**: The remaining value of your registered investments will be fully taxable in the estate of the last surviving spouse. When the first spouse passes away registered investments can be transferred to the surviving spouse without any tax implications. However, when the second spouse dies, all remaining registered investments are taxable as income. For example, if there were $500,000 of RRIF investments at the time of death, the $500,000 would be taxed as income. In this case approximately 40% of the value would go to the tax department.[4]

- **Non-registered investments**: These investments are deemed to be sold at the time of death. Any remaining capital gains will now be taxed. A capital gain is the difference between the current market value and the cost base of the investment account. The cost base is the amount of the original investment plus any interest or dividend income received minus any withdrawals. When

---

[4] Some provinces have surtaxes now.

the capital gain amount is determined, 50% of the gain is taxable at your marginal tax rate. For example, if the value of the remaining investment account is $500,000 and the cost base is determined to be $300,000, the capital gain is the difference between the two (in this case $200,000), 50% of which is taxable (in this case $100,000). This amount is added to your income and taxed accordingly. Odds are that 40% or more would disappear in tax.

- **Real estate**: Your principal residence is tax-free whereas other forms of personal use real estate are not. A common example of this is the family cottage. The cottage would be taxed in a manner similar to other non-registered investments. The amount of tax to be paid is based on the deemed market value of the property at the time of death. The amount that is taxable is the difference between the deemed market value and the cost base of the property. The cost base is the amount paid for the cottage plus any additional costs for renovations and upgrades. The difference between the market value and the cost base is the capital gain. Fifty percent of the capital gain is added to income in the estate. You can apply the Principal Residence Exemption to any property at this time, preferably the one with the largest capital gain (see below). Remember also that U.S. real estate may attract additional estate taxes in the U.S.

- **Rental properties**: During their use rental properties will have been depreciated for tax write-off purposes. This depreciation may be recaptured for tax purposes depending on the market value at the time of death, meaning the total amount taxable is a combination of the capital gain plus the recaptured depreciation.

- **An incorporated business enterprise**: An incorporated business enterprise is taxed in the same way as real estate and is subject to Capital Gains Tax.

Non-Taxable Assets

- **The principal residence**: The gain in value on the property you declare as your principal residence is not taxed when sold. You can declare any home to be your principal residence but you can only claim one home as your principal residence at one time. In some instances, if your cottage value has risen more than your city home, you may wish to declare your cottage to be your principal residence. You do not have to declare your principal residence exemption until the time of sale or death.

- **Tax-Free Savings Account (TFSA)**: The new Tax-Free Savings Account, launched in January 2009, can be very beneficial when planning your estate. The income, growth and capital gain value is all tax-free. The account enables you to invest up to $5,500 per year per spouse. If you do not invest the full

$5,500 in any one year, you can carry over the difference to the following year. If you withdraw money from the TFSA you can put back the same amount in the future. In other words, you re-create the available contribution room when you make a withdrawal.

- **Life insurance proceeds**: Life insurance proceeds are tax-free. Proceeds which are named to specific beneficiaries go directly to them, tax-free, and not through the estate, where the funds would have been subject to probate.

To pay the least amount of tax in the estate, you should minimize the amount of registered investments at the time of death in favour of tax-free proceeds such as the ones just discussed.

Tax Reduction Strategies

To reduce the tax in your estate, consider one or more of the following tax reduction strategies.

Charitable Giving

There is a great opportunity to reduce taxes through charitable giving. When completing the tax return for the estate, you can opt to make a charitable contribution up to 100% of the value of the year's taxable income. If, for example, the total taxable income in the estate is $200,000 then you could choose to give all of this income to charity. By doing so you are able to reduce taxes.

Another component of this strategy is to donate "publicly traded" securities to charities. This would eliminate the capital gains taxes on these securities while also creating a tax credit. To receive this benefit you must state in the Will that these securities are to be donated to a specific charity. Remember, however, that the total charitable gifts can be up to the total earned income in the year of death.

Use and Re-Create

Convert all RRIF income to an annuity, which acts like a pension plan. A lump sum of money is invested with an insurance company in return for a guaranteed lifetime income. Often the income received is greater than the RRIF income that was received before this conversion was made. In many situations most or all of the additional income received will go toward the funding of a new joint last survivor life insurance plan. The life insurance plan is paid to your beneficiaries on death. Because you have converted all of the RRIF assets to an annuity, when you die the annuity will end and nothing will go to your estate (unless you die within a guaranteed period that you selected at the time of purchase). This strategy uses all of the RRIF assets but then recreates these same assets for the beneficiaries. By following these steps you have a risk free lifetime income in retirement, no tax in the estate, plus a tax-free benefit paid to your heirs.

Life Insurance to Fund the Tax Bill

Another approach is to calculate in advance the expected tax bill in the estate and fund the tax bill with life insurance thus removing the burden from the heirs and leaving a larger legacy. Perhaps the tax bill is expected to be $300,000. You could purchase a joint last survivor life insurance plan for $300,000. The cost of the premium is dependent on your age, and you may be surprised at how low the cost will be. The insurance would be paid to the estate at the exact same time as the tax bill was due. This is another way you can minimize the effect of the tax bill on the estate, assuming the tax bill is something that you cannot avoid. We refer to this as "paying the tax bill" with fewer dollars since the cost to fund the insurance is much less than saving up the same amount of money over time.

Testamentary Trusts [5]

Once the tax bill is paid, you can pass on your assets to your heirs in a structure that could provide great tax benefits to them longer term. Let's assume that each grown adult child receives $600,000 of after-tax money inside of a testamentary trust. Income earned in the trust would be taxed on a marginal rate basis.

Let's assume that the beneficiary already earns an income of $50,000 and let's assume that the taxes paid would be approximately $9,707 (taxes will vary by province and for the type of income). If the beneficiary receives the inheritance personally, invests the money and then earns an additional $30,000 of interest income, the $80,000 of total income let's assume that the tax payer now pays taxes of approximately $19,985. This means that the $30,000 of interest income creates an estimated $10,277 of tax.

By comparison, if this same interest income was taxed inside the testamentary trust, the tax due may be closer to $6,615 (depending on the province of residence). This means that by receiving the inheritance inside the testamentary trust the beneficiary may be avoiding approximately $3,662 in tax each year. Over 20 years the total tax savings would exceed $73,000.

A testamentary trust is set up through the Will of the last survivor. The trust details can be flexible allowing all of the money in the trust to be drawn out if it was prudent to do so. Yet, by setting up the trust you have created a lifetime of tax savings on this money.

Note: By using a testamentary trust structure in your Will you are not reducing taxes in the estate. Rather you are reducing income taxes for your beneficiaries in the long term. Also note that these tax rules are currently under review.

---

[5] Some tax changes on the horizon

Topping Income up to Bracket

In Canada we live under a marginal rate tax bracket system. As you reach certain levels of income the next dollar of income you earn will be taxed at a higher rate. In some instances it is beneficial to take additional RRSP/RRIF withdrawals up to the next tax bracket level and invest this money into an after-tax account (ideally the TFSA). By doing so you avoid having the remaining RRIF assets taxed at a higher rate on your estate tax return. This point emphasizes how important it is to manage your tax return year by year.

If you do not consider closely who your beneficiaries will be, odds are the tax department will sneak in and be your largest beneficiary. Significant tax savings can occur when a charitable contribution is made, when tax-efficient investment vehicles are used, when you strategically use your principal residence exemption, and when you use life insurance to either expand your estate or to pay for the tax. Once the estate has been cleared, a testamentary trust can be used for the long term tax saving benefit of the beneficiaries.

> ***Whatever you do, don't leave a blank cheque for the***
> ***tax department.***
> ***Choose your beneficiaries wisely.***

Begin With the End in Mind

Steven Covey, in his bestselling book "*7 Habits of Highly Effective People*", writes of the benefits of "beginning with the end in mind". What does this mean?

If we know what we wish to achieve then we can work backwards to see what is needed to achieve the outcome. This chapter has highlighted several suggestions to consider:

- Minimize taxable investments in your estate.
- Use life insurance to pay the tax on those investments that are taxable in the estate with a substantially smaller financial outlay.
- Use life insurance to create tax-free proceeds for the beneficiaries.
- Apply the principle residence exemption to the property with the greatest capital gain.
- Consider the use of testamentary trusts in your Will.
- Consider using charitable contributions to reduce taxes owing.

The Survivor Analysis

Completing this analysis will illustrate the impact, both financial and otherwise, of the death of spouse A on spouse B and vice versa. Ask these questions:

- What are the terms of the Will?
- If Dad passed away first, what would be the financial impact on Mom?
- How will her income change?
- Is this enough income?
- What are the tax implications?
- What decisions should she consider if she needed more income at that time?
- What is her guaranteed income expected to be at that time?
- Does her guaranteed income cover her basic income needs?
- How does this situation change if Mom passes away first?
- What are the directions in Mom's Will? Should the Will be changed due to a change in circumstances?
- Where are the risks?
- What are the opportunities?
- What are the tax implications?

The Final Estate Analysis

The final estate analysis focuses on the tax implications, charitable giving and estate transfer plan when both spouses are deceased.

- What directions and bequests are included in the Will?
- How much tax is to be paid?
- How much money is to be transferred to the beneficiaries of the estate and what will be the impact to the beneficiaries from a taxation point of view going forward? Remember, if the bequest will result in a high rate of tax, the time to reduce this tax is now. If you are considering setting up a testamentary trust to reduce the tax effects on your heirs, it must be provided for prior to death in the Will.
- Are there strong desires to leave money to specific charities? If so, what are the tax implications of charitable donations and where should these donations come from? (i.e.: should any charitable donations come from individual stocks so as to receive more favorable tax treatment than cash?).
- Is there a way to enhance/increase the amount of the charitable contribution to reduce taxes payable and increase estate value for the benefit of the heirs?
- Is there a way to reduce taxes or pay fewer tax dollars through the use of life insurance?

- Are there specific assets that should go to specific individuals and why? Has this been communicated to all the stakeholders in the family?

- Do you wish to see your assets divided amongst your children in a particular way to avoid awkward family arguments?

- Who have you named as the Executor of your Will? Are all family members aware of this decision and are they comfortable with this? Your Will is often the last communication you have with your children. In many instances it is beneficial to have all children named as executors. One or two of the children may do the bulk of the work and some of the children may decide that they do not need to have signing authority after the fact, but naming them all as co-executors can be a step that will reduce family conflict.

One of the best ways to *Master Your Retirement* is to take the time to plan. Explore the risks and opportunities. Think ahead and "begin with the end in mind." Do this and you will Master the Final Outcome.

IN SUMMARY

The Final Estate Plan

THINGS YOU NEED TO KNOW

- Any remaining value in your RRSP or RRIF is fully taxable as income in the estate of the last survivor.

- Any remaining investment assets or real estate is subject to capital gains tax in the estate of the last survivor.

- The use of the Principal Residence Exemption eliminates the capital gain on that property. If the capital gain on the cottage is greater than the capital gain on your city home (over the same period of time), you may wish to apply your exemption to the cottage.

- The value of the Tax-Free Savings Account at the time of death is non-taxable.

- Insurance proceeds are non-taxable.

- You can contribute up to 100% of your earned income in the year of death to a charity.

QUESTIONS YOU NEED TO ASK

- At this moment, how much of your current estate would be taxable?

- How much tax would have been paid by the estate?

- Is there a way to reduce this tax?

- How much do you wish to give to charity?

- Is there a way to multiply this gift using life insurance?

- Is there an opportunity to withdraw additional RRIF assets (i.e.: topping up to bracket) to potentially reduce taxes owing in the estate down the road?

THINGS YOU NEED TO DO

- Create an estate optimization strategy for the next five years. The goal is to reduce potential taxes in the estate by taking certain steps today.

- Maximize annual contributions into the Tax-Free Savings Account.

- Keep track of the cost base of both the cottage and your city home. This will help to determine on which property to apply the Principal Residence Exemption.

- Consider the benefit of Joint Last Survivor life insurance as a way to "pay taxes with few dollars" or to multiply the value of your estate for charitable or other purposes.

DECISIONS YOU NEED TO MAKE

- Is it important to you to leave your affairs in good order?
- Is it important to you to maximize the value that goes to your kids, grandkids and to charity, while minimizing the amount that goes to government?
- Is it important to you to leave a lasting legacy?

Mastery Principle

Clean up your mess. Leave things better than the way you found them. The world will be a better place. Be detail oriented, anticipate the risks and be forward-looking.

CHAPTER

12

Managing Portfolio Risks

*"Personal development is your springboard to personal excellence.
Ongoing, continuous, non-stop personal development literally assures
you that there is no limit to what you can accomplish."* BRIAN TRACY

Sam and Susan retired two years ago. Over the past many years, retirement has been an important focus of their lives and, as a result, they have read many books on the subject.

They found that each of the books had important things to say, but they clearly noticed some differences. Some focused primarily on retirement living and lifestyle but spoke very little about the finances. Books written by portfolio centric advisors focused on issues of security selection and dividends whereas books written by financial advisors seemed to have a clear bias towards mutual funds, guaranteed minimum withdrawal products from life insurance companies and long term care insurance. They observed that most books ignored important aspects such as tax and investment fees.

Some books emphasized the importance of setting aside one to two years of income so that the portfolio could be allowed to grow, yet this is something that seemed very counter intuitive to Sam and Susan. Some emphasized the importance of drawing income from your mutual funds over time while others suggest that this should be the last thing you should do due to the negative impact of "reverse dollar cost averaging".

So much advice and yet no certain answers.

Sam and Susan are still unclear as to what the real risks of retirement are and how they can protect themselves.

THE ISSUES

What are the real risks of retirement and how do you address them?

Every author and every article written will have a different number. Some will say that there are four key risks while others will come up with 10. There is always some overlap between these lists, but to get better clarity we need to go back to where we began and take a look at the Great Killers of Wealth: taxes, fees, inflation, interest borrowing costs and market volatility.

Now, many authors will talk about things such as longevity risk (the risk of living too long and running out of money) and rising health care costs (which I discussed in a previous chapter and do acknowledge that it is a growing issue) but I believe that these issues can best be handled by first addressing the Killers of Wealth. For me, based on my life experience, it keeps coming back to the Killers of Wealth because once you deal with these issues the rest seem to take care of themselves.

This is similar to the discussion I had about long term retirement planning software. I can't help but conclude that if you take care of the short term, over and over again, the long term will take care of itself. However, if you ignore the important details in the short term (such as the Killers of Wealth), then the odds are less that the long term will result as projected.

We have already talked about taxes at length in this book. Now I'd like to talk more about managing the portfolio and minimizing investment management fees. In my view, you want to work with an investment advisor who is licensed in and able to offer you the widest range of investment choices, from GICs and bonds, to individual stocks, exchange traded funds and managed mutual funds. If the advisor has access to the widest range of investment products then you are most likely to have the best tool used for each situation. Needless to say, the "license" held by the advisor should be one of the first things you check out before investing with someone. My personal bias is that you want to work with someone licensed as a portfolio manager.

Having access to the widest range of products creates the opportunity to reduce investment management fees. As stated earlier in the book, investment management fees can range from 1.5% to 3% of the value of your portfolio each and every year throughout your retirement. Since you will have the greatest amount of wealth at retirement, you run the risk of also paying the greatest amount in fees. For example, if you have a $500,000 investment portfolio that pays an annual management fee of 1.5%, the annual cost is $7500 and over 25 years of retirement this total can rise up to $187,500. Does this number shock you? Well, now double it because the total money management fees for some products and portfolios is double this amount ($375,000!). If you had a $1 million portfolio, it could be double the fee again. Needless to say, this is a very big deal. So you want to look for an investment platform that strives to minimize investment costs.

Finally, you want to focus on managing volatility. Volatility is the degree to which the value of your portfolio rises and falls over a short period of time. Ideally, you want to have as little volatility as is reasonable for the objectives you wish to achieve. Remember, slow and steady wins the race. Now, the lower the investment management fees, the easier it will be to achieve your desired return with less risk. This makes it clear: if you have an investment portfolio with higher management fees, the manager needs to take more risk so as to achieve a higher return just to overcome the higher fees. In other words, there is no benefit to you until the manager achieves a return higher than the fee, yet they need to take more risk with your money to get there. In my view, there is no glory in risk and there is no glory in holding investments with higher investment management fees.

Many retired folk would like to live out their retirement vision in a manner that is as low risk as possible. I have yet to meet anyone who wanted to take on more risk in their retirement. Yet, what creates the most havoc for most retirees are situations or scenarios that catch them off guard. Many investors will say things like, "I didn't realize that what I was investing in had such a high risk." Usually, this statement is made only after the investment they were holding produced a significant negative return.

How can you find your ideal risk level? Start with a "benchmark", a standard to compare the other alternatives against. As the rule goes, "something is only as good as what you compare it to". If you don't have a framework in which to make a comparison, then it is very difficult to make an informed decision.

When we look at retirement planning, we need to create benchmarks for investment risk and return, income guarantees and taxation. Without these benchmarks you run the risk of being easily influenced by the next great investment idea or product concept.

In this chapter we will explore the important aspect of managing portfolio risk. When you understand how to manage portfolio risks, you are able to minimize the impact of market volatility and portfolio risk. This is consistent with Principle 5: The Importance of Managing Risks and Developing A Back-Up Plan.

THE SOLUTIONS

Understanding Risk and Return

What is a reasonable rate of return and how much risk does one have to take to achieve this return? Ironically, at the time of writing the first version of this book in 2008 we experienced a substantial market decline. These declines do occur and the timing of one's retirement date is critical.

First and foremost, it is extremely important to know that those who retire at the beginning of a market cycle have substantially greater odds of financial success than those who retire at the end of a market cycle. The year 2000 is considered to be the end of the last growth cycle (1982 – 2000). The period between 2000 and today, 2015 or even to 2020 will be considered to be a bear market or sideways market cycle. Those who retire during this period of time need to be cautious. If you do not modify how you approach your investments, you run the risk of seeing significant capital losses.

Let's look at what some of the long term averages tell us. A Balanced Portfolio, one that invests 50% in Canadian Bonds and 50% in Canadian stocks, over the last 25 years has seen an annual compound return of 8.3% (for the period ending July 31st, 2013, after fees). By comparison, the Canadian stock market has seen an annual compound return of 8.7%. With this in mind, what kind of long term portfolio return is reasonable and how much risk do we have to endure to get this return?

The Canadian Balanced Portfolio has seen one year annual returns range from a high of +28.4% to a low of -19.0%. If you are retired and drawing a regular income from this portfolio, and the value of the portfolio drops, you may never recover the money you have lost. If the value of your portfolio is $500,000 and you are drawing 8% per year (i.e.: $40,000) and the value of your portfolio drops by just 10%, the value of your portfolio at the end of the year would range between $410,000 (if you took out all of your income at the beginning of the year) and $432,000 (if you took out the income gradually throughout the year). To receive $40,000 in income the next year, the portfolio will need to earn 9.25% to 9.75% per year from this point forward just to maintain your income. To receive this higher rate of return, you will need to change your portfolio from balanced to an extremely high risk structure by investing 100% of your portfolio in the stock market.

One of the ways to measure risk is by using something called "standard deviation". Standard deviation measures the volatility of investment returns over a period of time. The higher the standard deviation, the higher the level of risk. Therefore, you would want to choose the investment with the lower standard deviation.

The difference in the level of standard deviation (i.e.: risk) between our neutral, balanced portfolio and the Toronto Stock Exchange (over the last 10 years ending July 31, 2013) is a whopping 89%. In other words, to increase the average rate of return from 6.8% to 8.3% (a 22% increase in the return) you will need to increase the level of risk and volatility by 89%!

Every investment has some risk. Investors must always be aware of the downside risks to a portfolio. It will be the one or two bad years that can quickly undo four to five good years. That is why you need to pay more attention to risk than return.

What is a reasonable long term return expectation? Based on 10 year historical data ending July 31, 2013, the average neutral balanced fund produced a return of +5.0% per year. So, to be conservative for estimating and planning purposes, use a range from 4% to 6%.

How much of your retirement vision should you put at risk?

With this basic understanding of risk and volatility, to what extent do you wish to have your retirement income exposed to investments that in the past have declined by as much as 10% to 20%?

Perhaps the answer to this question for you is zero. For others is may be 10%, 20% or 30% of total income. It is important to resolve this question to give you peace of mind in retirement. However, I clearly recommend that you never have more than 30% of your income rely on the ups and downs of an actively managed portfolio.

Understanding Long Term Average Portfolio Returns

What is a reasonable annual rate of return? Is it 5%, 7%, 10%? To answer this question, let's focus on the long term average rates of return of different types of portfolios over different periods of time. We focus on portfolios because our objective is to produce the highest possible return with the least amount of risk.

Considerable research has been conducted on this subject over the past 50 years. Building an efficient portfolio is similar to cooking a meal. Each new ingredient added, and the amount that is added, will either greatly improve or greatly detract from the quality of the meal. The same is true for an efficient portfolio. Each new investment added to the portfolio, and the amount of money placed into that investment, will either add or subtract risk while adding or subtracting return. The objective is to hold a blend of different investments that produce the greatest return with the least amount of risk at all times in the market cycle.

To understand long term average returns let's look at three sample efficient portfolios that have three different levels of risk: a conservative portfolio, a balanced portfolio and a growth portfolio.

	Conservative	Balanced	Growth
Canadian Bonds*	65%	50%	35%
Canadian Equities**	18%	25%	33%
Global Equities***	17%	25%	32%

* The Scotia Capital Broad Market Bond Index for Canadian bonds.

** The Toronto Stock Exchange Composite Index for Canadian stocks.

*** The Morgan Stanley Composite Index (in Canadian dollars) for global equities.

The above table describes three common portfolios: conservative, balanced and growth. In general each portfolio would have three components: bonds, Canadian equities and global equities. The bonds are the "defensive" side of the portfolio. That is why the Conservative portfolio has almost twice the amount of bonds (65%) as does the Growth portfolio (35%). The Equities component is the exposure to the stock market. Exposure to the stock market can be gained by investing in individual stocks or through other types of investments such as mutual funds. In general, we believe it is beneficial to divide your exposure to the stock market by investing half into Canadian equities and half into global equities.

When you begin to invest, you first need to focus on the amount of risk you are willing to accept. Do you wish to have a low amount of risk? If so, you are a "conservative" investor. Are you comfortable with a high amount of risk? If so, then you are a "growth" investor. Do you wish to take a middle of the road approach? If so, you are a "balanced" investor.

With this understanding, what has been the short, medium and long term rate of return for these three different types of portfolios?

The long term compound annual rate of return for these three portfolios is as follows. For comparison purposes, we will also look at the return of the Toronto Stock Exchange (TSX):

TABLE 1: Annual Rate of Return

	Last 3 Years	Last 5 Years	Last 10 Years	Last 15 Years	Last 20 Years	Last 25 Years
Conservative	4.2.%	3.5%	3.9%	4.3%	5.7.%	7.0.%
Balanced	5.0%	3.0%	5.0%	4.2%	5.6%	6.4%
Growth	4.9%	3.0%	4.9%	4.6%	6.3%	6.6%
TSX	5.1%	1.3%	8.3%	7.4%	9.0%	8.7%

Source: MorningStar PalTrak software for data ending July 31st, 2013.

What is a realistic rate of return expectation?

- A Conservative Portfolio (65% in bonds, 35% in equities): 4% to 6%.
- A Balanced Portfolio (50% in bonds, 50% in equities): 5% to 7%.
- A Growth Portfolio (35% in bonds, 65% in equities): 6% to 8%.

It is very important to understand that the rate of return for these types of investment categories will NEVER be the same year after year. There will be times when the returns for each of these categories will be higher and there will be times when they will be lower than the averages shown here.

Understanding Short Term Volatility and Risk

There are two sides to every investment: return and risk. It is easy to focus on returns, and when returns are good, volatility in returns or risk seems almost irrelevant. However, there is always a time throughout a typical market cycle where risk is the more dominant component of the investing equation. In 2008 all of the gains of the last 4 to 5 years were erased in a matter of months.

The challenge is how to quantify risk?

Risk can be measured by a calculation known as "standard deviation". Let's look at the long term annual "standard deviation" for the Toronto Stock Exchange. It will help us answer the question about risk. This is a very important concept as you will see in the next section.

To measure risk we begin with the long term rate of return. The Toronto Stock Exchange produced an average annual return of 8.7% over the past 25 years (Table 1). To achieve this return you had to take some risk. Just how much risk? Over the past 25 years (ending July 31st, 2013) the standard deviation of the Toronto Stock Exchange is 14.1% (Table 2).

If we add and subtract the standard deviation from the average return we see that 66% of the time the annual rate of return was between -5.4% and +22.8% (i.e.: 8.7% return + 14.1% standard deviation = 22.8%; 8.7% - 14.1 = -5.4%.) What does this tell us? It tells us that 2/3 of the time the one year return was likely acceptable to most people.

However, what about the other 34% of the time? The good news is that half of this time the returns were even better than the +22.8% noted above. The bad news is that 17% of the time the one year returns were worse than -5.4%. This is what I refer to as the "Red Zone".

The "Red Zone" represents those historical one year returns that would typically occur 17% of the time or once every 5 years. Just how bad did the returns get during this time? If we subtracted the standard deviation figure two more times from -5.4% we would see that there were occasions where the 1 year return was as low as -33.6%. This sounds a lot like the 12 month returns for 2008!

To truly understand risk, it is important to consider the Red Zone.

Let's take a look at the Red Zone for our three sample portfolios.

TABLE 2: Annual Standard Deviation

	Last 3 Years	Last 5 Years	Last 10 Years	Last 15 Years	Last 20 Years	Last 25 Years
Conservative	2.9	5.0	4.5	4.1	5.3	5.9
Balanced	5.0	8.2	6.0	7.2	8.2	7.8
Growth	7.0	10.8	7.8	8.9	9.3	9.1
TSX	10.5	16.5	14.6	15.3	14.8	14.1

Source: Morningstar Canada Paltrak Software. Ending July 31, 2013.

Here are the results for the Red Zone over the past 15 years:

- The Conservative Portfolio: The bottom 17% of returns were between -3.9% and -8.0% in any one year.
- The Balanced Portfolio: The bottom 17% of returns were between -10.2% and -17.4% in any one year.
- The Growth Portfolio: The bottom 17% of returns were between -13.2% and -22.1% in any one year.
- The Toronto Stock Exchange: The bottom 17% of returns were between -23.2% and -38.5%.

As you can see, a portfolio is defined, not by its return, but by its degree of risk 17% of the time. In moving from "conservative" to "growth" the downside risk becomes greater and greater. That is why it is critical to understand the asset mix of your portfolio and the degree of downside risk.

In your younger years, as you were building your wealth, you could sustain these downturns and keep on investing. Now that you are close to or are in retirement, protecting capital and purchasing power is of paramount importance. Before considering any investment you must consider the downside risk. It is extremely important to recognize that even the most conservative portfolio can lose money.

So here's the really big question: If you knew that there was a one in five chance that your conservative portfolio could drop by 8.0% in any one year, would you be ok with that?

By comparison, note that the balanced portfolio could drop by as much as 17.4% and the growth portfolio 22.1%. Obviously the growth portfolio is more volatile and aggressive than the conservative portfolio, but also note that the 15 year returns are virtually identical. So has it been worth it to take all of the risk of the growth investment over the past 15 years? Absolutely NOT!

Taking on more risk to generate a higher return will run the risk of encountering back to back years of significant negative returns. The negative return combined with the income withdrawal will significantly reduce the capital. It is possible that you may never earn this capital back and it will be lost forever. The income earned on this smaller amount of money will not cover your lifestyle income wants in the future. In an effort to meet your income wants, you have taken more risk only to end up with depleted capital. For some people, this has occurred in the first two to three years of their retirement, forever impacting their long term lifestyle options.

The best approach is to strive to have a low degree of risk at a modest level of income. If this isn't possible you may need to consider the purchase of an annuity for greater security, reduce expenses, work part time to supplement your income or postpone your retirement date.

The Importance of Portfolio Reviews

The last point about taming risk in your portfolio is to review your portfolio regularly from a pessimistic, moderate and optimistic perspective. A range of outcomes is always a wise consideration so as to keep your expectations at appropriate levels and to prepare for the unexpected. Every three to four months project your returns over the next three, six, nine and 12 months based on different scenarios. Calculate the impact of a return in the low 17% return zone (the Red Zone = the pessimistic view). Then, calculate the impact of a return in the typical 66% return zone (the moderate return). If markets and the economy are doing well, project the outcome of above average growth (the optimistic outcome). This exercise will help you understand the impact of different scenarios on your portfolio and your level of comfort with the risk you are currently taking. You may want to complete this exercise with your advisor.

If you do not do this, odds are you may be lulled into a false sense of security that the investments you own are of low risk when in fact that may not be the case.

IN SUMMARY

Managing Portfolio Risks

I've tried to demonstrate in this chapter that there is no glory in taking portfolio risk in retirement. In essence, slow and steady wins the race. Yet, many retirement plans will recommend that you take more risk in your portfolio so as to offset the long term risks of longevity, health care and inflation.

This is clearly the wrong advice in my view.

Alternatively, we go back to basics. By minimizing the taxes incurred and the fees paid on investments, you keep more of the money you invest. By investing in lower risk investments, you avoid the risk of losing capital through a widely fluctuating portfolio. This helps to preserve and grow your capital.

Some investments from insurance companies will offer a guaranteed minimum withdrawal benefit of 5%, for example. This income is guaranteed for life so you have very little risk of running out of money. To obtain these guarantees, the investor pays an additional fee of close to 1% (or more) of the value of the portfolio. You can now see that this is counter-intuitive. The higher the fees, the greater the risk that is often taken in the portfolio so as to achieve a greater gain. Yet, long term historical figures suggest that taking this extra risk is simply not worth it. In the end, you pay higher fees that are simply not necessary if you follow my prescribed approach: minimize taxes, minimize fees and ultimately lower the portfolio risk.

As a result, you sleep better at night knowing that your investments are safe, which in turn, can add to your health, peace of mind and sense of satisfaction.

THINGS YOU NEED TO KNOW

- Investment portfolios have risk; perhaps more than what you may be aware.
- For every percentage of additional return you desire, you will increase the level of risk threefold. Risk and return is not a one to one relationship.
- Ideally you want to have a low risk, conservative portfolio in retirement earning a 4% to 6% annual rate of return.
- You may never have as much money in your portfolio as you do today. Liquidity, tax efficiency, low fees and a reasonable investment return are the four key considerations of an investment.

QUESTIONS YOU NEED TO ASK

- How much risk are you comfortable with at this stage in your life?
- What percent of your income do you wish to have come from variable sources?
- Where are we in the economic cycle? Is the economy in recession? When is a recovery expected to start?
- How low could your portfolio go before you begin to feel uncomfortable?
- How liquid are your investments?
- What are the total fees of your investments and is there a way to reduce these costs?
- Am I chasing returns? Does the return in the portfolio demonstrate risk?

THINGS YOU NEED TO DO

- Evaluate the risk profile of your portfolio on a regular basis.
- Evaluate your comfort with risk on a regular basis.
- Evaluate the risk profile of the market on a regular basis.
- Evaluate how much risk you really need to take in your portfolio on a regular basis.

DECISIONS YOU NEED TO MAKE

- To what extent are you prepared to be actively involved in your portfolio? This does not mean that you would have to "do it yourself" but rather be involved and take an active interest with your advisor.
- To what extent would you prefer to implement the 100% guaranteed solution and avoid all of the ups and downs of the market?

Mastery Principle

There is no glory in portfolio risk. Focus on income first, and then design the lowest risk portfolio to generate this income. Never rely on engineered products to protect you from risks that may be impossible to protect against. Instead, evaluate your portfolio frequently in the context of your goals, the portfolio risk profile and the environment at the time. Anticipate the risks and develop a backup plan.

13

The *Master Your Retirement* Process

How to Fulfill Your Dreams with Peace of Mind

*"When you were born, you cried and the world rejoiced. Live your life
so that when you die, the world cries and you rejoice."*
CHEROKEE EXPRESSION

David and Kathleen loved reading the 2012 version of *"Master Your Retirement"*.
The information was very interesting and the ideas were nothing but stimulating.
But even with all of this provocative conversation, David and Kathleen were still
looking for an easy way to execute their plan.

David and Kathleen are well educated and they have done well for themselves over
the years. To be honest, however, they just aren't that interested in money related
matters. They want the most out of their money, but would prefer to spend only
the absolute necessary amount of time on this stuff and nothing more.

How can David and Kathleen Master Their Retirement in the simplest way possible?

THE ISSUES

When you break a larger problem down into its smaller pieces, the problem
becomes that much more manageable. Unfortunately, to truly *Master Your
Retirement*, to get the best value for your hard earned savings, to live the life you'd
most want to live, you do need to pay attention to the details. My experience tells
me that putting your retirement on auto-pilot, or selecting expensive investment
products that are designed to protect you from things that are impossible to protect against, is no answer. No, unfortunately, there is some work involved.

To make this work as easy as possible, I will break down everything we've learned into small steps that you can complete throughout the year, each and every year. No one piece is that difficult to manage. When these pieces are spread out throughout the year, you will accomplish a significant amount.

THE SOLUTIONS

Three Important Processes

There are three important processes I'd like you to consider as your "fast track" to Mastery:

1. **The monthly process**: In this process I have allocated specific activities for each month. By doing so, you achieve a lot over the year, but in smaller, simpler time slots throughout the year.

2. **The income layering process**: I have frequently referred to the importance of managing income and expenses. Consider these five steps as the most simple and effective way to achieve this goal.

3. **The portfolio review process**: As you know by now, I don't advocate putting your portfolio on auto-pilot. I will summarize three important steps to consider whenever you evaluate your portfolio, in May and September of each year.

These three processes apply each of the 7 principles noted in chapter 1. Remember, these are the principles that we see the Masters apply consistently throughout their lifetime.

Principle 1: Make Gradual Changes Over Longer Periods of Time.

Principle 2: Be Externally Focused.

Principle 3: Be Forward-Looking.

Principle 4: Work Together As A Team.

Principle 5: Quantify the Risks and Develop a Back-Up Plan.

Principle 6: Be Detail Oriented.

Principle 7: Never Stop Learning.

Think about how each of these principles are applied as you consider the three processes recommended below.

Process 1: The Monthly Process

Note: The Principles and the Rules mentioned below are from Chapter 2.

January: Focus on the Big Picture. Where do You Stand Today?

1. Update your personal net worth statement (Principle 4, Rule 1): January is a great time to update your net worth statement. In this way you will be able to see all changes over a calendar year.

2. Review your income and expenses (Principle 4, Rule 2): If you are retired, your RRIF payment, CPP and OAS payments will all have changed as of January 1. Enter these new figures into your budget and you will quickly see if more income is coming in than expenses going out.

3. Review the Great Killers of Wealth (Principle 4, Rule 3): To what extent were you successful last year in reducing taxes, fees and interest costs while addressing rising inflation and volatile markets? Are there any concerns at this time that should be addressed with your advisors?

4. Be forward-looking: The big picture (Principle 5): What phase of retirement are you in today? What would be the impact to your situation if you were to enter into the next phase of retirement in this current year? Do you need to consider a Plan B for any type of event that concerns you?

5. Review your portfolio: What were the returns for the previous year? What worked well? What didn't work well? What would you change?

February: Focus on Changes to Government Policy

1. Review government programs (Principle 4, Rule 4): In February and March each year, the Federal and Provincial Governments will announce their new budget as well as any changes to specific tax credits and government income programs. Most budget descriptions will be very specific in announcing "changes for seniors". Watch out for these headings so that you can be aware of current or future changes to programs and credits in which you currently participate.

2. Now is the time to make any final RRSP contributions.

March: Focus on Your Summer Plans

1. Be forward-looking: Prepare your summer lifestyle plan (Principle 5): What's the plan this year? Are you staying around? Are you travelling to the same or different location? Are you travelling with the same or different friends? How much money will you need to meet these plans and when will this money be needed?

2. Update your income and expenses (Principle 4, Rule 2): Does the timing of your expected expenses match the timing of your income? If not, how much

extra will you need and when will you need it? Be in touch with your financial advisor to begin discussing the most tax-effective way to draw this additional income.

April: Focus on Tax

1. Prepare your taxes: If you haven't done so already, prepare your tax return.

2. Review the previous year's tax picture: What was your marginal tax rate? Did you violate any of the clawback zones? Could you reduce taxes by changing the type of income you receive? Was income split equally?

3. Project your tax picture forward for the current year: Based on your projected income for the current year, what do you project your tax picture to look like? Will you be potentially violating any clawback zones? Will income be split equally? Are you withholding the right amount of tax on withdrawals? Review the tax picture again in November.

4. Adjust your income strategy: Do any changes need to be made to one or more of your income sources? Should withholdings be increased or decreased?

May: Focus on Your Portfolio

1. Review the current environment (Principle 4, Rule 5): What is going on in the world around you today? Is it time to "reduce" the risk profile of your investment profile? (More on this coming up in this chapter) Are interest rates rising or falling? Is the dollar rising or falling? What are stocks expected to do? Should you have this conversation with your advisors?

2. Make any necessary changes to your investment portfolio in preparation for the summer months.

June: Focus on Progress: Are You on Track for the Current Year?

1. Review your expenses (Principle 2, Rule 1): How are you doing so far this year? In January you updated your revenue and expenses when you knew what new sources of income were to come in. In March you updated your plans for the summer and reviewed your expenses again. How are you doing so far? Are you staying on budget? Are you unsure of where your money is going? Perhaps now is the time to check to make sure you are spending your money in ways that are consistent with your values?

2. Review the timing of expenses (Principle 2, Rule 2): When do you expect future expenses to arrive? Will you have the money available at that time to cover these costs?

3. Differentiate between needs and wants (Principle 2, Rule 3): Looking at your expenses today, is it clear to you the difference between your "needs" and your "wants". Are your needs staying modest? Are your "wants" consistent

with your values? Are you living the life you'd love to brag about and is this reflected in the way you allocate your financial resources?

July: Focus on You: Are You Living Your Year Like You Planned?

1. Review your lifestyle: Did you make plans for your summer? Are you now doing the things that you wanted to do at this time? Are you spending enough time with the people you most want to spend time with? Are you getting out of the house and remaining active?

2. Review your health: Are you on track to meet your health goals? How's your diet and exercise? What changes need to be made here? Do you need some assistance or support to achieve these goals?

August: Focus on Your Winter Plans

1. Be forward-looking: Prepare your winter lifestyle plan (Principle 5): What's the plan this year? Are you staying around? Are you travelling to the same or different location? Are you travelling with the same or different friends? How much money will you need to meet these plans and when will this money be needed?

2. Update your income and expenses: Does the timing of your expected expenses match the timing of your income? If not, how much extra will you need and when will you need it? Be in touch with your financial advisor to begin discussing the most tax-effective way to draw this additional income.

September: Focus on Your Relationships

1. Your spouse: How is the relationship with your spouse? Are you doing the things with your spouse that you'd most like to do? If you could change or add anything to this relationship, what would you do? What is one thing you could do to support your spouse in an activity that is important to him / her? What is one thing your spouse could do to support you in an activity that is important to you?

2. Your family: How is the relationship with your kids and grandkids? Are you seeing them as often as you'd like to? Would you like to plan a trip or a larger family gathering?

3. Your friends: How is the relationship with your various groups of friends? Are there any couples you'd like to spend more time with?

October: Focus on Your Portfolio

1. Review the current environment (Principle 4, Rule 5): What is going on in the world around you today? Is it time to "increase" the risk profile of your investment profile? (More on this coming up in this chapter) Are interest rates rising or falling? Is the dollar rising or falling? What are stocks expected to do? Should you have this conversation with your advisors?

2. Make any necessary changes to your portfolio in preparation for what is typically the strongest quarter of the year for equity markets.

November: Focus on Tax

1. Review your current year tax picture: How much income have you received from each source up to now? How much more are you expected to receive from each source? What would you expect your current tax picture to look like? Do any changes need to be made before December 31st?

2. Review your capital gains/losses: Do you have realized gains or losses from the current year in your investment portfolio or from a prior year? Should you realize any gains or losses from current investment holdings so as to minimize past, current or future taxes?

3. Did you turn 71 this year? If so, this is the last year to make an RRSP contribution. Should you make one last contribution at the end of December so as to maximize your current deductions?

December: Focus on Reflection: the Past Year

1. Review the past year: Looking back, how was the past year for you? Did you do the things you most wanted to do? Did you spend time with the people you most wanted to spend time with? What were the best decisions you made in the past year? If you had it to do all over again, what would you do differently?

2. Looking ahead to the next year: If you could change anything from the previous year what would you do? Is this something that is a priority for the coming year? If the coming year is to be "perfect" what does it look like?

3. Review the yearly budget: So how did the income and the expenses end up for the current year? Were there any unexpected onetime expenses? Are there any new expenses that began this year? Did the timing of your income match the timing of these expenses? Is there anything that you'd like to change for the coming year?

Summary

Hopefully you will agree with me, that when you break down a larger, more complex problem into smaller steps, the problem or the challenge does not seem so big any more. As a matter of fact, once you get through the first two years of retirement, you will find that this routine will become very simple and easy to manage. I would also expect that you will expand on the things you include each month because you see the benefit of this type of approach.

Again I wish to emphasize that this approach really costs you nothing but a little time. Compare this to the hundreds of thousands of dollars of costs that can be incurred with the Great Killers of Wealth and you can quickly see that this is time well spent.

To round out this chapter, I'd like to summarize the steps to be taken whenever you review your income and your expenses. I refer to this as the Tax-Efficient Retirement Income Planning Process.

Process 2: The Income Layering Process

You goal is to create a tax-efficient, low risk income that will in turn give you considerable choices, freedom and peace of mind in retirement. You achieve this outcome through the income layering process.

Step 1: Identify Your Sources of Income

What are your sources of income?

Make a list of all of your different sources of income. Identify those sources which are guaranteed and those that will fluctuate.

Step 2: Understand What You Spend

To fully understand what you spend, consider the following steps:

Make a list of everything that you spend money on today. Divide the list into two groups: a) expenses that occur every month and b) expenses that typically occur once every year. By dividing the list into these two categories you can now see the timeline for your expenses.

Next, classify the monthly expenses into two categories: a) basic income needs and b) lifestyle income wants.

Now you can begin to make some informed and important decisions. You begin to see how much money you really need to maintain your basic living needs. You also begin to see how much money goes towards those things that are nice to have, but not essential.

In most cases, people have enough (or more than enough) money to cover their basic income needs. Yet, many people may have just enough money (or not) to cover their lifestyle wants. An individual often becomes concerned about their finances and the fluctuation of either their income or their portfolio, when their lifestyle wants are at risk.

Are you better off trying to fund your current lifestyle with inadequate resources or are you better off adjusting your lifestyle to focus on those things that are most important to you within the boundaries of your available resources? It would be great to retire with more than enough money on which to live. However, with the volatility of the stock market and the fluctuations of the economy, you would need close to 20% more total assets just to buffer from these common occurrences. Now you not only need enough money to meet your peak lifestyle but 20% more.

Your retirement income plan must have flexibility and it must have a buffer. That is why it is so critically important to understand what you spend.

Step 3: Match Your Guaranteed Sources of Income with Your Basic Living Needs

Now that you have the figures for Canada Pension Plan, Old Age Security and your Pension Income, compare the total, after-tax monthly amount that you would receive with the basic monthly living expenses identified above. How close are these two numbers?

- Are your basic income needs covered by these guaranteed sources of income?
- How important is it to you to have your basic income needs covered by guaranteed sources of income?
- What percent of your total monthly income needs (basic needs + lifestyle needs) do you wish to have covered by guaranteed sources of income? 50%? 75%? 100%?

If your guaranteed income sources match or exceed your basic living needs, then you are on the right track. If not, then you may wish to consider converting some investment assets to an annuity so as to make sure all basic living needs are met through guaranteed income sources.

Step 4: Understand the Canadian Tax Structure to Get the Most from Your Friends in Government

As mentioned previously, it doesn't matter what you have, it only matters what you keep. The tax system, when used most efficiently, can make a substantial contribution to increasing your after-tax income.

Understanding the tax system is extremely important because it helps to answer the question: "If I need more money than the basic guaranteed amounts noted above, which source of income do I draw from first?"

By understanding the tax system you can strategically draw the right amount of income from the right source at the right time. By doing so you can maximize the dollars received from the different levels of government while also maximizing your after-tax income and minimizing the risk of the portfolio.

Step 5: Prepare for the Future

It is important to look one to three years down the road to ensure the decisions made today do not negatively impact your tax picture in the future. Plan ahead and do not put yourself in a situation whereby you are paying more taxes than necessary at any time in your life. If you do this each and every year, your plan will always be for the next three years. The extent to which you always get the short term right, the long term will take care of itself.

These five steps will help you become a Master of your income through all phases of retirement by layering your income in a tax-efficient manner.

Process 3: The Portfolio Review Process

In the monthly process noted above, I suggested that there are three specific times in which you will want to review your portfolio (January, May and October). Some may prefer to review and track the portfolio monthly, but I suggested January, May and October because these are the times of year in which changes in the "market environment" typically occur.

In this section I will share with you some simple strategies to manage portfolio risk.

1. **Be aware of the bigger picture trends**: What are the bigger picture trends today and how do these trends influence your portfolio? Are interest rates likely to rise or fall? Are energy prices likely to rise or fall? Is the economy growing or remaining flat? Are stocks likely to rise or fall? Now, I appreciate that the answers to these questions are not easy, but I do believe it is important to consider these factors before you invest. When you have a view as to the next six to 12 months, you can select your investments with confidence.

2. **The portfolio tilt**: When I speak about portfolio risk, my recommendation is you think in terms of "tilting" 20% to 30% of your portfolio towards those things that have a higher probability of growing in value and away from those things that have a higher probability of declining in value. The 20% to 30% "tilt" will follow the big picture trends (described above) and be modified throughout the year (as per the seasonality described below). You may tilt toward cash (in the spring) and equities (in the fall). You may tilt toward more commodities, real estate trusts and real return bonds if the US dollar is expected to fall or you may maximize your foreign investments if you believe that the Canadian dollar will fall in value in relation to other currencies. Note that a 20% to 30% tilt is all you need. If you tilt too much at the wrong time, you can get hurt. If you tilt too little at the right time, you will always benefit. This is all about "managing risk" rather than squeezing out significantly higher returns. Remember also that most of your returns, from the actively managed portfolio, will often come from pure dividend income. This component of the portfolio will remain as is over time. The

"trading portion" (i.e.: the 20% to 30% tilt) is all that is needed to help you manage the risk profile of your portfolio.

3. **Do I need to take this risk today**? Do you already have enough income to cover your expenses? Is your portfolio growing year over year? Are you living within the 30% test? If so, then do you really need to take this risk today? What is this risk?

Personally, I believe that this is one of the most important questions all retirees should ask at all times. With this being said, however, it can be a challenge to know which risks are for real and which risks are not.

This is the same as the equity markets and the economy. It is not any one event that causes a market collapse, but rather an accumulation of events, the timing of which is always difficult to predict.

As a result, most of the growth or decline in the stock market, when measured over years, actually happens over a matter of days. Some research has suggested that if you were to miss the 10 best performing days in the stock market over the past 10 years, your total rate of return would be cut in half. However, when you turn this around and take out the 10 worst days over the past 10 years, your rate of return skyrockets! This tells us two things: i) the actual growth in the stock market occurs over very few days over a very long time and ii) missing the 10 worst days (by being cautious when risk levels are high) will add more return to your portfolio. Most advisors do not pay close attention to the day to day or seasonal cycles of the stock market and thus recommend you always remain invested. However, if missing the 10 worst days actually adds greater returns, what strategies could you use to miss these 10 worst days?

The first way to "protect" against the 10 worst days is to structure a lower risk portfolio, based on the fact that you have a more tax-efficient income and a portfolio with lower management fees.

The second way to avoid the 10 worst days is to ask yourself "do I really need to take this risk today".

The third way to reduce this risk is to understand the seasonality of markets.

4. **The seasonality of markets**: The following material is drawn from the Thackray's 2010 Investors Guide, a book which I highly recommend to everyone. The book is a great analysis of the ebb and flow of the markets over time. With this information in hand, you can make small changes to your portfolio throughout the year so as to minimize portfolio risk.

• **The annual seasonal stock market cycle**: Some refer to this as "sell in

May and go away". Mr. Thackray refers to this as the Six'n'Six Strategy: Take a Break For Six Months: May 6th to October 27th. In this example, keep in mind that your portfolio is a combination of different types of investments. For the component of your portfolio that is focused on the stock market, consider the following information. Mr. Thackray has looked at the seasonality of the stock market cycle and discovered the following: i) from 1997 through 2008, the best time to be in the market was from October 27th through May 6th each year, ii) the total gain on a $10,000 investment was $164,551 (when you invest for the winter months and then hold cash for the summer months) versus a loss of $4362 (when you invested over the summer months and held cash for the winter months) and iii) Over this 32 year period, the winter months out performed the summer months 77% of the time. This is why I suggest that taking half or more of your equity positions off the table around May 6th may be a simple and prudent approach to minimizing risk. The number of negative summer months over this 32 year period was 15 or 47% of the time. The number of negative winter months over this 32 year period was seven or 22% of the time. When the summer months produced a negative return, the average return was -10.24%. When the summer months produced a positive return, the average gain was +7.4%. By comparison, when the winter months produced a negative return, the average return was -7.5% (27% lower average downside risk when compared with the summer months). When the winter months produced a positive return, the average annual gain was +14.98%, or double the average gain for the summer months.

As previously suggested in the monthly calendar section of this chapter, by reviewing your portfolio in May and October, you can adjust your portfolio accordingly to take advantage of this type of seasonality. From a portfolio perspective, all this may mean is that you hold a stock market index exchange traded fund (E.g.: ishares TSX 60 Index, for example) for the October to May period each year and then hold cash from May through October. This is a very simple trade to do each year to avoid the time of year when investment returns are typically less. All that this means is that you are investing more aggressively when the odds are on your side of producing a strong, upside positive return.

- **The relationship between growth and value:** Mr. Thackray also did a study on different types of management styles. This is a common definition in the world of mutual funds and pension managers. Some money managers are considered to be "growth" managers while others are considered to be "value" managers. There has been a constant battle between which is the better style of money manager. As you would expect, both are good, but at different times. Mr. Thackray's research suggests that the best time to focus on "growth" styles is beginning in October each year. The reason for this is because the fourth quarter, more often than not, is the higher performing quarter for the stock market each year. Therefore, a very simple "tactical trade" to make each year is i) invest with a "value" style from January through September then ii) invest with a "growth" style from October through December. Again, this is a very simple trade to make each year using either your favorite mutual fund managers or lower cost exchange traded funds. Mr. Thackray looked at US data from 1979 through 2008. By following this strategy, the average yearly gain would have been 13.2%. This strategy worked favorably 63% of the time. By comparison, the returns on the S&P 500 averaged 9.2% per year. This is a very simple strategy that you can use to increase your returns by close to 44% over the market return. Of course, it is important to note that the return on the Average US equity mutual fund, over the past 25 years (1986 – 2011) is only 5.4% per year after fees. This simple trading strategy, executed twice a year (in January, and September) outperformed the average US equity fund by almost 2.5 times.

- **Horizon's Alpha Pro Seasonal Rotation Exchange Traded Fund**: Mr. Thackray has incorporated many of his seasonal investing strategies into an investment that you could buy. The purpose of the fund is to invest into those areas, throughout the year, that have the highest probability of success, based on historical trends. Since inception the returns have been similar to the overall Toronto Stock Exchange, but at a significantly lower level of risk.

  You can have history on your side when you follow the historical seasonality of investment markets. In other words, you don't have to guess and you don't have to go it alone. All you have to do is spend the time, each January, May and October.

5. **Employ a creeping stop loss strategy**: A "stop loss" is an automatic sell order. If the investment you hold drops below a particular price, the sell order kicks in and the security is sold. A stop loss can be placed on any stock or exchange traded fund, but cannot be used for mutual funds. A "stop loss sell order" typically remains active for a period of 30 to 40 days, and then expires and needs to be reactivated.

   It can be very helpful to employ a "creeping" stop loss strategy. Every month, review each of your stocks and exchange traded funds. As they rise in value, raise the level of your stop loss order. By doing so you are better able to protect your past gains from sudden or unexpected market declines.

You can do this on your own, with your own actively managed discount brokerage account, or you can do this with your investment advisor.

My point is simply this:

- Focus more on risk management than total rate of return. Your returns will come when you first manage the risks.

- You can earn just as much return, if not more, by protecting from market declines when the risks are high than staying fully invested throughout the highs and the lows of the market.

- You can protect your capital by thinking in terms of a 20% to 30% tilt. This means that 70% to 80% of your portfolio will remain as is throughout the year, but that 20% to 30% will be tilted toward the highest probability outcome at that specific point in time.

- You can protect your capital simply by asking "do I really need to take this risk today".

- You can protect your capital by following seasonal market trends by either i) moving in and out of the market every May and October and ii) following the seasonality of the "growth" and "value" strategy.

- You can protect your capital by using a creeping stop loss strategy.

There are many types of strategies to follow, but my belief is that it is better to focus on these types of issues, two to three times a year, than it is to do nothing.

Doing nothing produces a random result, and your retirement period is too important for randomness.

IN SUMMARY

The *Master Your Retirement* Process

So much can be achieved when you pay close attention to the details, when you follow a series of rules and when you overcome the Great Killers of Wealth. In the end, it's really not that hard. In fact, it's just a matter of following a process.

When we began this journey together, I asked you the question: Are you prepared to put in the effort to potentially create hundreds of thousands of dollars of additional income in retirement? Hopefully now your answer is clearly 'yes'. Hopefully now you see how these benefits can be achieved.

In the end, everything worthwhile in life requires effort. You could go as far as to say that the three most important aspects of life are i) one's health, ii) one's relationships and iii) one's financial affairs. In each of these three areas very little is taught. But to achieve good health, you have to have a strong daily discipline of diet and exercise. To achieve healthy relationships, you have to work at them each and every day. The same is true for your financial affairs. To have clear choices in life, you need to spend time on your money. It's impossible to delegate your health and fitness to someone else, and still be healthy. This is obvious when you look at the number of people who gain weight again once they end their diet programs. It's impossible to delegate healthy relationships to someone else when you're constantly working late at the office. It's also impossible to delegate your financial affairs to someone else, who may be limited in what they can do for you based on their license alone. It's impossible to delegate the risk management of your financial affairs to a product or to a money manager that you never meet.

And this is my point. Retirement is complex. But by following some simple steps, you can achieve some amazing results.

THINGS YOU NEED TO KNOW

- By spending a few hours each month on your financial affairs, you can achieve some amazing results.
- There are three processes to follow: i) the monthly process, ii) the income layering process and iii) the portfolio review process.
- Financially engineered investment products are typically designed to fill a need based on issues that arose in the recent past. They are not necessarily the ideal product moving forward.

QUESTIONS YOU NEED TO ASK

- Are the investments I select 100% liquid? Can I get out of them at any time?
- Do I have the right team of advisors to work with?
- Is this something that my spouse and I can work on together?
- Which areas of the 12 month process are easiest to implement today?
- Which areas of the 12 month process am I not doing today but would be beneficial to add?

THINGS YOU NEED TO DO

- Take the first step. It is always better to start somewhere and then add as you go.
- Make a list of the 12 Month Process. Then read the book again and add more notes under each section.
- Open last year's tax return and evaluate it based on the Income Layering Process.
- Evaluate your current portfolio according to the Portfolio Review Process.

DECISIONS YOU NEED TO MAKE

- To what extent are you prepared to follow the monthly process?
- To what extent are you prepared to take the time to model your retirement income on the tax return?
- To what extent are you prepared to spend a little extra time monitoring your investments?
- Is it worth it to you to spend this time so as to potentially add hundreds of thousands of dollars of income over your retirement years?

Mastery Principle

Progress begins with the first step. Apply each of the seven principles consistently over time.

Epilogue

As we draw to a close this third edition of *Master Your Retirement*, I can easily and confidently expound, advocate and reinforce the power of the ideas, processes and principles contained in this book. Yet my dominant thought at this time always goes back to the question: what if things don't quite turn out as planned? Whether this be due to lower than desired or expected investment returns, higher than desired levels of portfolio risk and volatility, an illness, a job loss or significant unexpected expenses, I think we can all agree that things will never quite turn out as planned. So what do we do then?

It is with this question in mind that my attention in this edition of this book has turned to the importance of the "back-up plan". Whether it be in during your working and child raising years or during your retirement years, it is always comforting to know what the back-up plan will be just in case things don't quite turn out as planned. Where will the income come from should your income start to decline? Which expenses will need to be trimmed? Will we need to turn certain "non-income-producing assets", such as a cottage or a vacation home, into an income producing asset?

When I think of most of the clients I serve today, the vast majority have other additional assets or resources that could be sold and thus used as a future source of income. In some of these same situations, spending is likely to decrease in the coming years which may in turn help to offset declines in the value of an investment portfolio. We have yet to see anyone ever run out of money in their retirement, because there always is a back-up plan. The key, however, is to be aware of what this back-up plan is likely to be and at what point it would be initiated? When this is clear, then this often brings greater peace of mind, which refers back to some of the key points I wanted to make in this edition of the book. When you know what your back-up plan is likely to be, then you can have the freedom and confidence to plan your current, ideal, well balanced life as discussed in Chapters 1, 6 and 8. In situations where little to no "buffer" exists, then these people may choose to work longer or until such time as both OAS and CPP become available.

In light of the performance of the investment markets over these past 10 years, it is also important to say that your investment plan is one of the most important components of your overall success in retirement. Yet, the investment markets today remain anything but predictable. Taking on too much risk may reward you with higher returns from time to time, but put you at risk of seeing sizeable declines in the value of your capital. Taking less risk may protect you from these declines, but may also result in a lower return that guarantees a loss in capital over time. The question is: what is the middle ground approach? Hopefully I've address some of these issues in Chapter 12. This is definitely one of the major challenges facing retirees today.

All of these issues go back to my point about thinking of your life as a series of stages and phases. We will all go through the 5 phases of retirement, which means that it is really important to reflect on your overall plan in 3 to 5 year increments at a time. We have found that this is often the best approach to keeping things on track, managing risks and developing a good back-up plan.

Finally, as I stated up front, my goal and passion in life is to help other people be confident, comfortable and happy. I firmly believe that this comfort comes with information, knowledge and education. I hope you found this edition of *Master Your Retirement* to be extremely helpful in identifying both the risks and opportunities in today's retirement reality and I hope you found it inspiring to take your next steps with confidence. I would like to leave you with a quote from Napoleon Hill: "Ascertain what you like to do best, and do it as a labor of love with your heart and soul." This, I believe, is the road the happiness, passion and peace.

Doug Nelson

Technical Appendix

Numbers You Need to Know from the Tax Return

- Old Age Security:
  - For those born prior to 1958, you will have the option of receiving your Old Age Security benefit at age 65. For those born between March 1958 and February 1962, you will receive your Old Age Security somewhere between age 65 and 67, depending on your month of birth. For those born after February 1962, you will receive your Old Age Security beginning in the year you turn age 67.
  - Old Age Security payment amounts are reviewed every 3 months and increased based on the rate of inflation.
  - The current benefit amount (Q1 2014) is $551.54 per month.
  - This amount begins to be clawed back if income exceeds $71,592 (2014). This is clawed back at a rate of 15% for every dollar of income above this threshold amount.
  - You can elect to defer receiving your OAS amount to age 70. This could be very beneficial as your benefit amount will increase by 7.2% for every year of deferral. This is the equivalent of earning a guaranteed 7.2% rate of return. This may beneficial especially if you have other sources of income that, when added together, exceed the OAS clawback level at 65. Between ages 65 you could purposely choose to draw down these other sources of income so that by age 70 you are no longer at risk of a clawback. At that time you would receive a larger OAS amount which may in turn provide greater financial security for the balance of your life.

- Canada Pension Plan amounts:
  - The maximum benefit available in 2014 is: $1038.33.
  - Remember that your benefit amount is based on your contributions during your working years, less any adjustments for low income years or child rearing years.
  - If you begin to draw your CPP retirement income benefit in 2014 and you are under age 65, your CPP pension benefit will be reduced by 0.56% for every month prior to your 65th birthday. For example, if you are 60 in 2014 and you begin to draw your CPP pension benefit, a discount of 33.6% will be applied the benefit you were scheduled to receive at age 65.
  - In 2015 this figure will increase to 34.8%. In 2016 this figure will increase to 36%.
  - Due to the size of deduction for drawing your CPP prior to age 65, we believe it is best to defer drawing your CPP until age 65. This, in effect, provides you with a guaranteed return of 6.5% to 7% per year. If your rate of return on other investments is lower than this amount, then it may be prudent to draw income from your lower return investments first so as to allow your CPP benefit amount to grow.
- The Basic Personal Amount:
  - This figure represents the basic amount of income you can earn before you pay any tax.
  - There is a basic amount when calculating the Federal amount of income tax and there is a basic amount when calculating Provincial tax, which is unique to each Province.
  - These amounts are indexed annually, however, some provinces do not index on an annual basis.

The table below represents the 2014 amounts.

Federal	NL	PE	NS	NB	ON	MB
$11,138	$8,578	$7,708	$8,481	$9,472	$9,670	$9,134
	SK	AB	BC	YT	NT	NU
	$15,378	$17,787	$9,869	$11,138	$13,668	$12,567

Source: www.taxtips.ca

- The Age Amount:
  - This is available to individuals who are age 65 or older at the end of the taxation year.
  - The Federal portion of this credit is $6916 in the 2014 tax year. This amount is deducted from your taxable income each year, thus reducing your tax payable by approximately $1037, per spouse.
  - To receive this credit, your income needs to be less than $34,873 in 2014. This is applied to each spouse. This is why it is very important to split income equally in retirement, so as to maximize the potential benefit from this credit each and every year.
  - If you were able to maximize this credit each year for 20 years in retirement for each spouse, this would be a potential tax savings of $41,480. This number would actually be higher because i) these benefits are indexed with inflation each year and ii) a similar credit is applied to the provincial tax return.
  - However, the extent to which your income exceeds the clawback threshold of $34,873, you will begin to lose the age credit amount. The age credit amount ($6916) is reduced by 15% of net income (line 236 of your tax return) above $34,873 (for 2014). The credit is completely eliminated when income exceeds $80,980 (for 2014).

- 2014 Federal Personal Credit Amounts: The following credit amounts are available on the tax return. Remember that there is also a similar credit available on the Provincial Tax Return. Most of these amounts are also indexed annually:
  - Basic Amount: $11,138.
  - Spousal Amount: $11,138.
  - Age Amount: $6,916.
  - Disability Amount: $7,766.
  - Caregiver Amount: $4,530.
  - Infirm Dependent: $6,589. (which includes the Family Caregiver Amount).

- TFSA Contribution Limits:
  - 2013 limit: $5500.
  - 2014 limit: $5500.
  - 2009 – 2012 annual limit: $5000 per year.
  - Total maximum contribution room available per spouse: $25,500.
  - 2014 additional contribution room: $5500.

- Note: if you take money out of the TFSA in 2014, you can put this money back into the TFSA in the following tax year.
- RRSP Contribution Limits:
  - 18% of your earned income in the prior year, less any pension adjustment values.
  - The maximum contribution room for 2013 is $23,820. The maximum contribution room for 2014 is $24,270.

Bibliography

Canadian Census 2006

Canada's Aging Population 2002, Health Canada

Covey, Steven: *7 Habits of Highly Effective People.* Winnipeg Free Press, 1989.

US Census Bureau

Colvin, Geoffrey. *Talent Is Overrated: What Really Separates World-class Performers from Everybody Else.* New York: Portfolio, 2008. Print.

Hill, Napoleon, and Matthew Sartwell. *Napoleon Hill's keys to success: the 17 principles of personal achievement.* New York: Dutton, 1994. Print.

Staying Ahead of the Curve, a 2007 National Survey

Journal of the American Medical Association

Morningstar Paltrak Software

http://www.knowledgebureau.com/index.php/programs-courses/courses/elements-of-real-wealth-management, 2014.

Index

KNOWLEDGE BUREAU
NEWSBOOKS

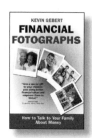

Financial Fotographs
How to Talk to Your Family About Money
By Kevin Gebert

"I wish my parents had talked to me about money." If this resonates with you, you are not alone. Millions of families have a difficult time embracing financial conversations so crucial to the ongoing health of family income and capital. This is especially true in times of transition: changes in health, career or retirement.

If you are raising a young family and challenged with how to teach principles for healthy money management, this book's for you! But if you are in your mid-thirties and wondering how to broach the subject of your role in the financial future of your ailing parents, you'll love this read, too.

Empower Your Presence
How to Build True Wealth With Your Personal Brand and Image
By Catherine Bell

"Presence" has always held a certain mystique that is empowering and attractive – it can improve relationships, transform situations, and influence success.

Whether starting out in your career, asking for venture capital, meeting potential clients, or advancing into a new social environment – including retirement – you will want to stride forward with confidence and ease. EMPOWER YOUR PRESENCE is about developing that distinctive quality that can create opportunities and propel you to new heights.

This is a must-read book for ALL generations – Gen Y (18 to 33), Gen X (34-48) and Boomers (49+) – who want to invest in their best attributes, passions, and skills and market their unique promise of value as an important part of their ongoing personal success.

Jacks on Tax
Your Do-It-Yourself Guide to Filing Taxes Online
By Evelyn Jacks

"Do-it-yourself" is back in vogue and that applies to your tax preparation as well. More Canadians are looking for ways to save money and this year, you can save time and money understanding your own return and take better control of your financial affairs too, with Canada's most trusted, best-selling tax author, Evelyn Jacks. Do you know what you don't know? When to talk to a pro? This book will help guide you, line-by-line. It's a book for everyone because its premise is simple: a more informed taxpayer, working with a collaborative professional community, will get more out of the tax system now and in the future.

Financial Books to Help You Grow and Preserve Your Wealth
At leading bookstores or order online at www.knowledgebureau.com